Michael Zabec

10 Steps to High Definition Selling

A Service of

BuilderBooks™
National Association of Home Builders
1201 15th Street, NW
Washington, DC 20005-2800
(800) 223-2665
www.builderbooks.com

Ten Steps to High Definition Selling
Michael Zabec

Theresa Minch	Executive Editor
Jenny Lambert	Assistant Editor
Sharon Hamm	Copy Editor
Justin Stewart	Cover Designer

BuilderBooks at the National Association of Home Builders

ERIC JOHNSON	Publisher
THERESA MINCH	Executive Editor
DORIS TENNYSON	Senior Acquisitions Editor
JESSICA POPPE	Assistant Editor
JENNY LAMBERT	Assistant Editor
BRENDA ANDERSON	Director of Fulfillment
GILL WALKER	Marketing Manager
JACQUELINE BARNES	Marketing Manager
GERALD HOWARD	NAHB Executive Vice President and CEO
MARK PURSELL	Executive Vice President Marketing & Sales
GREG FRENCH	Staff Vice President, Publications and Non-dues Revenue

ISBN 0-86718-552-X

Cataloging-in-Publication Data
Zabec, Michael, 1946–
    Ten steps to high definition selling / Michael Zabec.
        p. cm.
Includes index.
    ISBN 086718552X
    1. Selling. I. Title: 10 steps to high definition selling. II. Title.

HF5438.25.Z33 2003
658.85—dc21

2002156748

Disclaimer
This publication is designed to provide accurate and authoritative information in regard to the subject matter covered. It is sold with the understanding that the publisher is not engaged in rendering legal, accounting, or other professional service. If legal advice or other expert assistance is required, the services of a competent professional person should be sought.
    —From a Declaration of Principles jointly adopted by a Committee of the American Bar Association and a Committee of Publishers and Associations.

For further information, please contact:
BuilderBooks™
National Association of Home Builders
1201 15th Street, NW
Washington, DC 20005-2800
(800) 223-2665
Check us out online at: www.builderbooks.com

4/03 E Design Communications/Circle Graphics/Victor Graphics 2500

This book is dedicated to my wife, Dianna,
and my children, Lori, Jason, and Josh,
who understand that
quality time sure beats quantity time.

About the Author

Michael T. Zabec is Executive Vice President of Homeview Contractors, Inc. He has been involved in sales for the past 35 years, has been Salesman of the Year too many times to count, and has been doing motivational speaking throughout the United States for a number of different sales organizations. He has taught sales to people who now own their own companies and have incomes of more than $500,000. Michael hosts an award-winning radio talk show called *Your Home, Your Views* on Baltimore's WCBM 680. He is well known in the sales field and considered to be among the industry's best in-home closers.

Acknowledgments

First and foremost I would like to thank my lovely wife Dianna and son Joshua for sharing me with this project. Their love and patience—and sometimes impatience—guided me through the task of writing. My wife was a believer in me before I was thoroughly convinced that I could provide a happy home and family. Thirty-six years later, three children, two grandchildren, and one on the way, she is still by my side. She is either a glutton for punishment or she really loves me. My world really would be nothing without her.

I would also like to thank members of the Homeview Contractors Inc. sales force for allowing me to be a part of their lives and giving me the food for thought that was utilized in writing this book. I would also like to thank them for their input during sales meetings, which generated a new thought process that gave me the ability to write down for the first time on paper exactly how and why the Ten Step Sales Plan should work.

I would like to thank Sheldon Forchheimer, my partner, my friend, and above all my mentor. He opened his heart and his business to me and allowed me to do the things I needed to do for the company. He has given me a new strength and a renewal of belief in others and myself. This book would have never come into being if it weren't for the acceptance of a business relationship with Homeview Contractors, which has provided me with a new lease on life. Thank you Sheldon.

I would also like to thank our marketing administrator, Val Seifert, for his continued support and friendship, always by my side in all of my business ventures. Val is one of my closest friends because he encourages rather than discourages, compliments instead of criticizes, and above all respects instead of disrespects. He has spent hours reviewing the manuscript and offering suggestions as to what might work a little better. He is definitely a major player in my life and will continue to be for as long as I am able to work.

I would like to thank my son Jason for all of his words of wisdom and all the years he has been with me in the sales field. I'm proud to say that he has been Salesman of the Year for three consecutive years. Most people see their children once in a while. I have watched Jason mature in the sales game, and his talents are far superior to most out there. He has not only listened to my words, he implements them on a daily basis. He has made me very proud.

I would like to thank Bob Hoppa, my co-host on *Your Home, Your Views* on WCBM 680. I would like to thank Bob for also being a true friend. I'm blessed to have two best friends when most people don't have any. Bob has given me praise and the strong will to continue when I was willing to set it all aside. This man has played an important part in my life and has gone through the growing pains with me as to establishing a long-term relationship. I would trust this man with my money, my family, my life. He has been a true inspiration and a very dear friend.

Last but not least, I would like to thank God for giving me my faith in myself and being with me each and everyday. You see, God already has control over my life.

Thanks to anyone I may have missed, and may God Bless.

Contents

Introduction

The days of brow beating potential prospects into submission during a close are gone. Confidence Sales are in, and hopefully here to stay. This book is not for the people who want to learn high-pressure selling tactics, but people who take pride in their product, in their company, and in themselves. If you currently work for a company that is not of these ethics, quit.

I can't run a business, but I can make a business run. Six years ago Sheldon Forchheimer threw the reigns of Homeview Contractors in my hands and said take it from 1.7 million to 4 million. This year we will net in excess of 6 million dollars in sales. We did not accomplish this by teaching our sales representatives high-pressure selling techniques or leaving the prospect's house with blood on the walls. We taught them to educate the prospect so that they will have a better idea of what they want when it comes time to purchase. We taught our sales people to sell our product to the exclusion of all other products out there. We emphasize the *trade up by trading down* theory.

Homeview Contractors specializes in prime replacement windows and replacement doors. We take the shopping out of the prospects' hands by searching all over the United States and finding the very best products at excellent prices to fulfill their needs. Part of selling is telling, and if you don't have a great company story, you may find it very difficult to close deals. People want high quality products that they can rely on with great guarantees.

I personally would rather apologize for the price once than the quality of the goods forever. That's why it pays to sell top-of-the-line goods. As we say, our windows are made in Cleveland Ohio, not in heaven, and they are made by human beings, not by angels. We definitely make mistakes, but the difference between us and everyone like us is we own up to them. No one is infallible. Many people believe they are, and the problem comes when they want you to believe it.

This book will give you insight on how to promote your product through confidence selling. You will enter into a new realm of professional selling with new words and a renewed commitment, which will bring in greater dollars for effortless selling. You will receive phone-ins and referral business simply because people want to deal with you. You will become an honest, upfront, stand-alone kind of person.

I have been an in-home closer for the past thirty-five years. I have sold vacuum cleaners, sewing machines, washers and dryers, televisions and stereos, carpet, fencing (vinyl and galvanized), refrigerators, freezers, lawn mowers (riding and self-propelled), and snow blowers. I have learned many ways to close deals and none involve high-pressure sales. Sometimes you must use a velvet hammer to get a prospect to move, but when I'm done, I expect them to be 100 percent satisfied.

I believe strongly in the Ten Step Sales Plan and use it in every selling situation. The reason I use it is because it works.

Entry

- Positivity Breeds Possibility

- Forget Your Prejudices

- Change Sell to Invest

- Persistence Breaks Resistance

- Respect Competition

- Insecurity Feeds Hostility

- Be a Leader

- Set Worries Aside

- Define Your Goals

- Try New Things

STEP 1

Entry

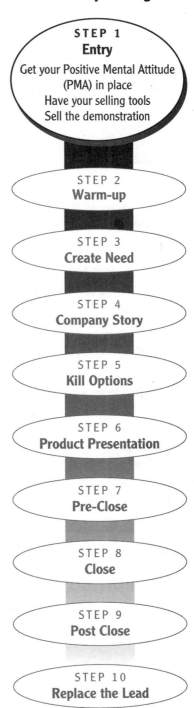

STEP 1
Entry
Get your Positive Mental Attitude
(PMA) in place
Have your selling tools
Sell the demonstration

STEP 2
Warm-up

STEP 3
Create Need

STEP 4
Company Story

STEP 5
Kill Options

STEP 6
Product Presentation

STEP 7
Pre-Close

STEP 8
Close

STEP 9
Post Close

STEP 10
Replace the Lead

Positivity Breeds Possibility

We salespeople are confident, positive, enthusiastic, and generally well liked. Sometimes when we enter a home, we are the most positive thing that has happened in a long time to the people we meet there. We definitely can become a positive force in the homes of people used to listening to negative newscasts and having negative interactions with others.

We are more than a breath of fresh air. We also carry a certain amount of charm and charisma that can mesmerize prospects and put them into a hypnotic state when we induce the ether of the positive sales presentation. At the same time, to avoid a recission, or sales cancellation, we must be careful to button the close up. Otherwise, when we leave the home, the ether can wear off, together with the clients' great

SALES PRO TIP

Positive Attitudes Create Possibilities
When you first walk up to the prospect's door, remember to maintain a positive mental attitude because you don't know what is behind the door you are about to knock on.

intention of making that buying decision, and they now wish to cancel.

Remember that you are there to sell a demonstration, and only a demonstration—nothing more, nothing less. If the prospects like what they see, they can call you back. They might even tell a few of their friends about the product and how much they liked it.

Job Interview Mentality

Think of entering your prospects' home as if you are going to a job interview. Whenever you approach prospects, you enter into the wonderful world of being interviewed for a job. Whether you get the job is entirely up to you, and how well you present yourself and your product. Remember that you probably are not the only person applying for the job. Your prospects have probably interviewed a number of people for the product they seek to purchase.

SALES PRO TIP

View New Prospects As Job Interviews
Treat every sales presentation as a job interview. Remember that prospects have other people in mind to sell them product. You must be on your best behavior, you must be polite, and you must make sure they understand that you want the job. Whether you get the job is entirely up to you, and how well you present yourself and your product.

As in a job interview, you must be on your best behavior. When you go to a job interview, you do things differently than you normally do. You represent yourself differently. You must say the right things, at the right time, and you must make sure the prospects understand exactly why you—and your product—are better than the other people who have applied for this job. You listen more attentively. You are more polite than you have ever been. You are more respectful of the person you are interviewing with. You maintain complete composure, along with that beaming smile.

And that's exactly how to conduct yourself during any sales situation. You must think of it as an interview. You must clearly translate to the prospects how badly you want this job, and how the product you have to offer is much more beneficial than anything else on the market today. You must talk about your resume, and about the other people you have satisfied—your reference list.

Remember that the prospects are the ones who will make the decision of whether or not to hire you. You must make them want to hire you. They will base their decision on how well you convince them that you are better than all the other people they have interviewed.

This interview process starts with the entry. Remember: if the prospects had already made their decision, you wouldn't be there.

Forget Your Prejudices

We sometimes have a tendency to do the worst possible thing a sales representative can do; that is, we prejudge a selling situation,

SALES PRO TIP

Keep Smiling
When you walk to the door, you are armed merely with a smile. Keep smiling as you introduce yourself and your company. Smiling is contagious, so use it to your advantage. If prospects tell you to hit the road, at least they might do it with a smile on their faces.

and we prejudge prospects—how they look, whether or not they are financially able to afford our product, or whether or not they are credit worthy. Prejudging can become prejudice.

Let's stop here for one second. You see, you are a sales person, not a banker, and "You are there to sell a demonstration, and only a demonstration—nothing more, nothing less."

As a sales representative, one of the first things you must do is to have a total understanding of your prejudices. Those prejudices might include short people, tall people, people of different origins, people who talk too fast, people who talk too slow, heavy people, skinny people, pipe smokers, engineers, and so on. And once you understand your prejudices, you must lay them all aside.

Sit down and write all your prejudices on a piece of paper. Before you enter any prospect's home or approach any prospect, read that list to re-familiarize yourself with your prejudices. This way, you will prepare your subconscious mind not to react, while keeping fresh in your mind exactly what your prejudices are.

Always remember this: I have walked out many times on prospects who I prejudged and later found that my inclinations were absolutely false. And the most frustrating part of such experiences is when I later pass those prospects' homes and find out that they bought a product from someone else. And to add insult to injury, they also got it on a payment plan through another lending institution.

As salespeople, we need to understand that we are neither mind readers nor soothsayers, and so our goal must be to treat every sales call the same, and not prejudge. Have I mentioned "You are there to sell a demonstration, and only a demonstration—nothing more, nothing less"?

The Two-Minute Drill

When I walk to the prospects' door, I think about the process I call the *two-minute drill*. I have two minutes from the time I meet those customers for them to form an opinion of me. First impressions are lasting impressions. Many sales are lost at the door because of bad vibes between prospects and the sales representative.

Whenever you first meet your prospects, understand that all of us have a little devil on our shoulder. This little devil constantly whispers things in our ear, such as "These people aren't going to buy anything; let's get out of here!" or "These people are deadbeats; you'll never get them financed." You must keep control of this little devil or he will ruin you.

For example, when the prospects first answer the door, they might inform you they "are not interested in purchasing anything at this time." This remark acts as an arrow that penetrates your heart and starts to bring you down. The devil uses this opportunity to jump on your shoulder and immediately try to talk you into bailing out. Bailing out under such circumstances is called *burning the lead*, a habit you never want to develop.

Remember: "You are there to sell a demonstration, and only a demonstration—nothing more, nothing less." (You will read this statement several more times in this chapter because it needs to be clear in your mind.)

The prospects might go on to say that "you are just wasting your time because we have no money and can't afford it even if it were free." Now the little devil on your shoulder is going into a seizure trying to talk you into blowing off this lead.

There, I said it again: blowing off a lead, burning a lead. Now forget that I did. Do not put these words into your sales vocabulary. More importantly, if you say them, don't ever do them.

Change Sell to Invest

As we've said, the entry is used primarily to sell the product demonstration. It is important for you to establish the fact that you are not there to sell the prospects anything. "You are there to sell a demonstration, and only a demonstration—nothing more, nothing less."

If you have a great product, you would not be *selling* to them anyway; you would be asking them to *invest*. Let's get rid of those naughty four-letter words such as *sell* and *cost*, and change them to *invest* and *investment*. The product you are selling is actually an investment that will pay for itself in years to come. A great product is one about which you can say, "You can invest in this product today, and in 7 to 10 years it will pay for itself."

All of these things are part of your entry—how prepared your thinking process is as a sales representative, and your ability to justify your being there.

The Wall of Resistance

I walk to prospects' doors expecting something called an initial *wall of resistance*.

Most sales are made when you encounter an initial wall of resistance at the door. The wall of resistance represents certain things prospects say on entry, such as "You're wasting your time," or "I told that lady on the phone I wasn't interested," or "I really can't afford anything now."

Most salespeople read such responses or prejudge these selling situations to mean the prospects are not interested in what you have to present. Instead, understand and expect these kinds of responses, and arm yourself with this philosophy: "Nothing a customer can say or do will discourage me from making a complete and thorough presentation."

The toughest people at the door, those who put up that wall of resistance, are generally the easiest people to sell. Their toughness is saying to you in hidden words, "*No*, I don't want to see what you have because I'm afraid I might buy it."

Many sales representatives will put their foot in the door so people won't slam the door on them. I like to stick my head in the door, so if they slam the door, my head will still be inside and I can continue talking.

Once you're inside the house, you've completed the first step of the sales plan, the entry.

Buyers Are Liars

We can elicit all the information we want from our prospects, but we must understand an old saying: "Buyers are liars." They rarely tell you the truth, for a number of different reasons. The major reason is that they simply don't have to. They owe you nothing. Because they are the customers, they are always right. And you are a guest in their home. If they had other estimates on a product like yours, why would they need or want to divulge this information to you?

Let me give you an example that demonstrates when prospects will lie. Let's say you do ask if they have ever received any other estimates. They tell you *No*, because when you ask them to buy, they can then tell you they still need to get other estimates. This is called a *stall*.

Now let's say you get mini-commitments from the prospects throughout the presentation, and you ask them things such as "If you were ever to do business, does our company sound like the type of company you would want to do business with?" and they tell you *Yes*. Then you ask, "If you were ever going to purchase a product, would this be the product you would invest in?" and they answer *Yes* again. Then, when you ask them to buy, they tell you they want to shop around. Shop around for what? They already told you that they want to deal with your company, yours is the product they want over every other product, and they want to shop around. They lied.

How can tell you tell if prospects are lying to you? The answer is a little-known secret: when their lips are moving. Always remember this secret, and you can't go wrong.

I'm not saying that it is wrong for prospects to lie. I am saying it is wrong for the sales representative to lie. You don't have home field advantage, and it's their ball. Prospects play the sales game, too, and that's OK.

Persistence Breaks Resistance

You must be persistent to break the resistance. My theory is "Be nice till you quote the price." That doesn't mean you should then become belligerent or a jerk; you just get serious about what you are doing. The hard sell is a thing of the past. Closing strategies do not include winning a battle but losing the war.

When little kids want something, they will often nag Mom and Dad till they finally give in. Children understand extremely well that being persistent will break the resistance.

What I mean by *closing* is simply conveying to the prospects that your product is superior to any other product on the market today. The hard part is that you'd better mean what you say, and it had better be true.

Simply put, you need to sell your product to the exclusion of all other products. What does this mean? It means you must know your competition. "He who knows the most controls the selling situation," and "The ABCs of selling are Always Be Closing."

If you went to an auto mechanic, and he told you your fagowee shaft needed to be replaced, that doing so was a life-or-death situation for you, and you knew nothing about automobiles, you would probably replace the shaft. Why? Because "He who knows the most controls the selling situation."

If we are not medical doctors and we don't know about medicines, we will take drugs a doctor prescribes, even if we don't understand the side effects this drug may pose. All we usually want to know is whether the drug will make us better. Why? Because "He who knows the most controls the selling situation."

Respect Competition

Early in the entry, prospects may bring up other products. The first thing one must learn as a salesperson is not to bad-mouth another salesperson's product. There are ways to discourage people from

purchasing another product without slamming it. People disrespect those who take other people—or their products—to task.

You can offer a solid explanation of why your product can be better than some other product similar to it; for instance, the way your product is manufactured, or the material that is used. For example, think about tool and dye costs in the manufacture of a product. In a comparison between your product and some other product, you could say:

> You see, Mr. and Mrs. Prospect, our product is manufactured a little differently than the other product you were looking to purchase. We invested a lot of money in the tools and dyes we used to manufacture this product because we wanted it to last longer, have little or no service problems, and keep you a satisfied customer forever. If the other company had the funds to do so, it would have made all the changes necessary to build its product just like ours. But that company goes by an old philosophy: "If it ain't broke, don't fix it."

You follow up a statement like this by saying:

> Mr. and Mrs. Prospect, if this is not going to be a long-term thing, and you really don't want to get the best bang for your buck, maybe you should consider purchasing a less expensive product.

Notice what I said: "You should consider purchasing a less expensive product."

> You see, our product is an investment, not an expenditure. Our product will pay for itself in the years to come, not end up costing you money. The bottom line, Mr. and Mrs. Prospect, is that price buyers are twice buyers. You can do it once, or you can do it twice; it's entirely up to you.

These statements ring true in the prospects' minds and establish instant credibility between you and them. You are confident of what you are saying, and prospects sense that.

Insecurity Feeds Hostility

Presenting the product that you want people to invest in is using the same systematic approach that the entire sales plan is based on. You present things in an orderly fashion, one piece at a time, and make sure throughout that process that you are covering each step of the sales plan.

A sure way to take the wind out of any sale is something I call the *I=H Factor*. Simply put, this means that if you make somebody feel inferior or insecure, they will come at you with hostile reaction. And it's important to recognize that the *I=H Factor* can include martyring or blaming other people for situations caused by oneself.

Try this little experiment. Tonight when you get home, when your loved one greets you at the door, rub your hand across the top of the door jamb, look at the dirt in your hand, and say, "Gee, Honey, don't you ever dust?" (Before you do this, though, make sure you have running shoes on and earplugs in place.) Insecurity breeds hostility, and that's a fact.

The bottom line is that you must keep your composure with prospects. Don't say anything that they can construe as controversial or opinionated. and leave religion and politics at the door. People hate opinionated people, so don't come off as one.

Whenever I want to make a statement, I start by saying, "Let me preface this by saying 'In my opinion . . . ,'" and then I go on to finish the statement. This approach takes the edge off the conversation and hopefully keeps me from being considered opinionated.

Be a Leader

It was once said that leaders are born, not made. But all the leaders and losers I know went through the same birth process. Leaders become leaders because they understand behavior modification, and they constantly work on it. Leaders start life the same way everyone else does. They drink milk out of a baby bottle, they learn to crawl before they can walk, and they generally start their learning process with their parents' guidance.

Let's suppose a child's parents aren't leaders. Are we to assume, then, that the child will not be a leader? Consider that we are all creatures of habit, and until we choose to break bad habits, they will remain with us forever. Human nature seems to be to take the line of least resistance.

Real leaders, however, learn to break their bad habits, and then they teach others how to break theirs. You see, leadership is something that starts out the same way for everyone. First, they go through the learning process, then they implement what they have learned, then they teach what they have learned, then they advance.

Think about being trapped in a mine with 10 other people. Would you be the person to get the ball rolling to find a way to escape? Would you be the one who says, "Listen up people; let's get a plan together. Here's what we are going to do"? You see, the greatest challenge in such a situation is waiting for a leader to emerge.

In sales, the situation is similar. Every salesperson can and must be a leader in the field of selling. You must learn to control your destiny, and then you can be confident of how you will learn to lead.

As a leading salesperson, you must clearly identify to prospects exactly why you are in their home and what you will be doing there. Next, you absolutely must provide a clear and concise product demonstration to achieve your ultimate goal, closure of the sale. You also need to think about selling your product. You must give prospects some idea of what your product will retail for. This is called *price conditioning*, and you'll learn about it in more detail later in the book. And remember that you don't want prospects to go into sticker shock when they hear the price. So you see, you must lead the entire presentation, starting with the entry.

SALES PRO TIP

To Succeed, Learn To Lead
At all times, you are the leader, and your primary responsibility is to keep control of the selling situation. If you lose control, you lose the sell. You must determine where the prospects sit, the flow of the presentation, when to hand out the pieces, when to pre-close, when to close, when to post-close. This is the road map to a successful sell.

You control the pace of the presentation. You control the flow of the words that go into the presentation. You control where the people sit, when you should talk low, when you should increase your volume, when you should ask the prospects questions, how much time you use on any piece of your product that you wish to demonstrate.

Throughout the sales presentation, you are in control, which makes you the leader. People follow the leader, so get them to follow you by a complete and thorough product presentation.

To succeed, you must learn to lead. And know that anyone can learn to be a leader, simply by using behavior modification. Salespeople must fight complacency, which is the real reason we don't accomplish all we set out to accomplish.

Set Worries Aside

Too often, sales representatives carry their personal problems with them into the prospects' home. When you knock on that door, you must be able to make your problems disappear, at least for the next two or three hours.

I have learned a simple way to do this. Every day that I have worries, I set them aside until, say, Thursday at 5 p.m. On Thursday at 5 p.m., I lock myself in my office, and from 5 p.m. to 6 p.m., I worry about all the things that I have to worry about. I have found this to be the most boring hour I spend all week, because all the worries I had have already been solved or have disappeared.

Whenever I'm driving and worries start to chew at me, I merely say to myself, "This is something I need to worry about on Thursday from 5 p.m. to 6 p.m., and my worries go away. With that in mind, I walk through the prospects' door worry free.

If you follow this system, you will be the most surprised person in the house when you get to the close and the prospects lie right down. When I trained sales representatives, I followed the system to a T, closed the deal without a hard sell, and the trainees would say in amazement, "Do they give you *all* lay downs?" The system is a wonderful thing—it works. Use it, don't abuse it, and never deviate from it.

Set Goals

Imagine, if you will, a ship leaving the dock on a voyage for Bermuda in the Atlantic Ocean. The ship has no navigational equipment and no charts. How long do you think it will take to get to Bermuda, and do you think you will ever get there?

The idea is the same in selling. If you don't have directions, and a plan for how you propose to hit your goal, you too will end up lost.

Before you enter the prospects' house, you must have a goal. Many people predict outrageous things they think they can do, and then they are only disappointed when they don't accomplish them— because they didn't have clearly defined goals.

I'm often amazed in sales meetings when I ask sales representatives what their goals are for the month. They frequently seem to come up with extremely high numbers that they have never before obtained. Sure, it's good to have high hopes, but it's also important to be realistic when you're setting a goal.

Making up a number is easy, but to accomplish that as a goal is quite a different thing. People tell me all the time what they think they can accomplish, but when it gets right down to it, they often fail miserably on the doing part.

SALES PRO TIP

There's an Ocean Between Say and Do
Whenever you make commitments, remember that action is required to carry out whatever you have committed to. Don't utter false commitments based on unrealistic predictions.

When you realize that there truly is an ocean between say and do, you can set more reasonable goals and not set the mark so high it is out of our reach. Remember that you shall be held accountable for your words and judged by your honesty and credibility.

You can't hit a target you can't see. You can easily set a goal if you first know *how* to do so. To set a goal for a month, first figure out how much money you anticipate you must have to take care of your financial obligations, and the extra you need to buy something special for your loved ones and yourself.

Next, you need to know how many selling days you have to accomplish your goal. Then you need to estimate how much you can do a day in sales, and then account for fall off, people not at home, and getting no demos.

You'll need to explore your customer base to see whether you can strategically squeeze more prospects in if necessary. Then you will calculate the total daily dollars you can sell, and multiply that figure by the number of selling days to arrive at what you have set your goal to be.

Next, you need to track progress toward your goal daily to make sure that you don't have to incorporate more time or prospects into your equations.

You must check constantly in this process to make sure you're on stride. You need to regularly evaluate where you are in respect to where you want to be.

You must have notes in your car reminding you of your goal. You must write the goal on your mirror in your bathroom with lipstick, for example, to remind yourself.

You must repeat your goal to yourself, and you must believe it. Remember: "The body manifests what the mind harbors."

And if you fall behind, don't give up. Double your output, and do some things that you don't normally do.

The Body Manifests What the Mind Harbors
Your thoughts control your destiny. If you are positive by nature, you will be posi-tive in your thought process, and your outcomes in life will be positive. Unfortunately, if you are negative by nature, the reverse will be evident. Think doom and gloom, and you shall be granted your wish.

Try New Things

As salespeople, being able to program ourselves to do new things that we don't normally do is probably the greatest challenge of all. That's because we are afraid to fail.

To learn to succeed, we must to learn to fail with dignity. So many of us fail and never give it another go because we feel less than competent and lose faith in ourselves.

But if our lives were just a series of victories without failures, we would not truly appreciate those sweet victories that bring out the leadership qualities from within.

Be a Farmer

You are no longer a salesman; you have just become a farmer. That's right, do some things you don't normally do. What does a farmer do? He plants seeds, of course. And that's your job, my friends. If you want to reap what you sow, you must plant seeds. Tell every person you speak to what you do, and that when they are ready, you will show them your product.

If only 1 person out of 50 calls you back, you're still way ahead of the game. You see, out of the 50 seeds you planted, 1 seed turns out and grows, and it's up to you to harvest it. You must also find time to water it, which means calling prospects back to see how they are growing, and to add fertilizer, which simply means to reiterate what your product will do for them.

The Power of Motivation

Consider the following examples, and ask yourself what the difference is between them. I'm conducting a sales meeting with about 30 people in the room, and I ask this question: "How many of you think that you could leave this room right now, without leads, and sometime between today and tomorrow morning write an order for $10,000?" Maybe one or two hands go up.

Now consider the same situation, except that I rephrase the challenge by saying, "If I offered you $1,000 pure cash to write an order for $10,000 sometime between today and tomorrow morning, how many of you think you could do it?" Every hand in the room goes up.

The interesting part is that 9 out of 10 times, 26 out of the 30 people will come back with a $10,000 order. Amazing, isn't it?

The reason for such results is that these salespeople will go above and beyond the call of duty and do things completely out of the ordinary for them, because they have extra motivation. For $1,000, they will do everything in their power and pull out all stops to meet the goal and deadline. They will sell friends, family, and any person who walks, wobbles, or creeps.

These salespeople will finally *experience* the theory "Nothing a customer will say or do will discourage me from making a complete and thorough product demonstration."

Now comes the sad part. If these salespeople had written the contract normally, they would have made more without the challenge. They would have made $2,000 in commissions at 20 percent, instead of $1,000. And they also would have made an additional 5 percent, or $500, for developing the lead themselves. (This is called a *self-generated lead*.) So in actuality, they lost $1,500.

To succeed in sales, you must apply a dollar value to any action you take that could result in a sale. Even though the money is not in your hand, you must visualize it there. If you do this daily, you will become a top-notch sales representative and a high-volume producer.

Self-Motivation

To be a high-volume sales producer requires constant self-motivation. Ways to motivate yourself include listening to motivational tapes, reading motivational books, and most important, hanging out with positive people instead of negative people and downers. You only gain knowledge by the books you read, the people you meet, and experience.

Sir Isaac Newton once said, "Objects in motion tend to remain in motion; objects at rest tend to remain at rest." For successful sales, you must keep in motion everyday, add one more positive habit, motivational practice, or sales technique, to your daily ritual, and before long that behavior will become habit.

Likewise, every week, do something you used to do—you know, one of those things that worked so well you stopped using it.

Refine your skills daily, and change you presentation often. And remember that the entry is the single most important phase of the selling presentation. Also, before you meet prospects, remember that you must continuously repeat this statement to yourself: "Nothing the prospect will say or do will discourage me from making a complete and thorough presentation."

If you can't get in the door, you can't sell your product. Once you're inside, you now have a number of tips and techniques to help you close the deal.

Warm-up

- ● Get Comfortable with Prospect

- ● Gather Information

- ● Take Control of the Atmosphere

- ● Lower Their Resistance Shields

- ● Build Trust

- ● Remember Questions are the Answers

- ● Defer Objections

STEP 2

Warm-up

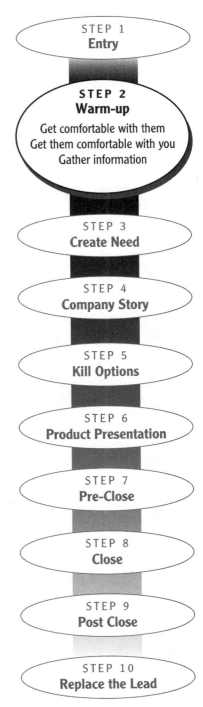

STEP 1
Entry

STEP 2
Warm-up
Get comfortable with them
Get them comfortable with you
Gather information

STEP 3
Create Need

STEP 4
Company Story

STEP 5
Kill Options

STEP 6
Product Presentation

STEP 7
Pre-Close

STEP 8
Close

STEP 9
Post Close

STEP 10
Replace the Lead

Get Prospects to Like You

During the warm up, you must get yourself to like the prospects, so that the prospects will like you. If you can get prospects to like you, they will listen to you. If they listen to you, they will buy from you.

So how do you get prospects to like you? It's easy. Compliment them on something you like about them. You can say many things to get prospects to like you. For instance, you can compliment them on their intelligence, their personality, or their taste in fine furniture. You just need to make them feel good about themselves.

Let Prospects Talk

Make a point of getting people to talk to you. If you hear the sound of your voice too much, you are not doing a very good warm up. The more prospects talk, the closer they

SALES PRO TIP

Compliments Work

Two gentlemen were standing at an intersection near a busy street. Another gentleman walked up and said to one of them, "I really like your tie."

The gentleman who had been complimented reached up, stroked the knot in his tie, and, feeling good about himself, said to the man beside him, "That was a really nice man; I liked him."

The picture of the man who had given the compliment was in the paper the next day. He was Jeffery Dahmer, a serial killer. Although Dahmer had never before met the gentleman wearing the tie, he observed and formulated an opinion about the necktie and complimented the man on it. Based on that compliment, the gentleman was convinced that Jeffery Dahmer was a likable person.

become to being your friend. The closer they come to being your friend, the closer they come to listening to you. You see, friends listen to friends. And if they listen to you, they will buy from you. So the closer you come to making prospects your friends, the closer you come to closing the deal. And if there are two individuals, make sure to make and keep eye contact with both of them.

Fact-finding questions are key to keeping prospects talking during the warm up. Open-ended questions are also important here. For instance, instead of asking, "Do you like living here?" (which would bring a *Yes* answer), ask the open-ended "What do you like about living here?" Get it? Open-ended questions keep prospects talking. Close-ended questions, which can be answered in one word—*Yes* or *No*—do not belong in the warm up. They have their place, which you'll learn about in a later chapter.

SALES PRO TIP

Act Like the Guest Host of the Tonight Show

When you enter the prospects' house, remember to change from salesman to guest host on the Tonight Show. A good guest host asks questions and elicits information.

God Gave Us Two Ears and One Mouth
Remember: this combination is so we can do twice as much listening as we do talking!

Find Something to Talk About at the Door

I have found a great way to get the people talking to me. After I have met the prospects, I say something like "I never would have found you without my GPS."

They start right in and say, "That's the navigation system that tells you how to get places, isn't it? I want one of those. Before you leave, maybe you could show me how it works?" This is an example of what we call the ice breaker, and it works very well to get people to start talking.

Here's another example. If I see a motor home or boat when I arrive at the prospects' home, I might say, "I see you people are avid boat enthusiasts. I had a boat, and I really miss it." Boom. You're in a conversation that the prospects can speak fluently about. Because I own a motor home, I especially like seeing those; I can really warm up to another motor home person. But if you don't own one, don't bring it up unless you say something like "I always wanted one. Are they fun and worth the money?" Now your prospects become the experts. They feel great about that, and they will probably talk for hours if you let them.

I also look for motorcycles, racing cars, travel trailers, or beautiful property. When I get to homes that are on beautiful property, I always use the phrase "You people live in a little bit of heaven." But I say that only if I really feel that way.

You never want to pick out something to talk about, however, that might relate to only one of the prospects you're meeting—something such as bowling trophies or other personalized things. You see, if the man is the one who won those trophies, you will spend your entire warm-up time talking to him, and you will lose his wife. She has heard these stories too many times before.

Enough Is Enough

During the warm up, you must know when to break off the small talk. In general, the warm up should last for as longs as it feels comfortable, and you will know when it is time to get to business. And even though sometimes you might feel like you could converse all night, that would be a mistake.

There are several ways to end the small talk. If you are selling windows, you would simply make a statement such as "You are really great people; I could talk to you all night. But let me ask you a question. Are the windows in this room the same as throughout the rest of the house?" If you are selling encyclopedias, you might say, "You are really nice people, I could talk to you all night. But let me ask you a question. When you need some valuable information from reference materials, how do you go about securing that information?"

SALES PRO TIP

When All Else Fails, the System Prevails

Engrain this thought in your head. Your goal is to put the 10-step selling plan to use as quickly as you can. The sooner you do, the sooner you will start to earn the big bucks. If you want the plan to work effectively, you must never deviate from it.

The more you do the sales plan, the easier it becomes to reach down deep and pull out words that will lead prospects into placing an order with you today. Every step of the plan is essential to bring the sale to a close. When in doubt, get all 10 steps out.

Use the Sales Plan—No Matter What

Use any way you can to casually introduce your product to the consumer. Don't let prospects throw you off by saying things such as "You're not going to go through that whole book are you?"

Stick with the sales plan, which you should know by heart. If your prospects become adamant with you, close the book, tell them you are going to give them the short version, and go through the plan exactly as you would if the book were open. The sales plan is the only system that works.

Many people in the business try to sell a product without explaining how it will benefit the prospects. Often, the problem is that we used to do things that worked so well we stopped using them.

For example, when we were first learning about the product, we were more successful selling it because we explained as we learned, and everyone understood what we were talking about. Then, as we refined our presentation, we skipped the simple explanation and went more in depth about exactly what we were selling. Over time, we become so knowledgeable about our product that we expect prospects to know exactly what we are talking about, and we end up talking over their heads. The problem with this is that going into long, technical, highly educational conversation sprinkled with statistical facts and figures is like Albert Einstein explaining the theory of relativity to a kindergarten class.

Your real job is to explain the product in laymen's terms, keeping the details as simple as possible. Use questions such as "Can you see how this would help you?" or "See how that works? Do you understand it? If you don't understand, please tell me, and I will try to be more explicit."

As you explain, paint pictures in the customers' minds of what you are saying. And make sure that prospects are participating in your presentation. Keep them involved by handing them parts and pieces. Prospects will not understand or appreciate a one-sided presentation in which the sales representative completely dominates. If you do this, you will lose the sale.

Trade Up by Trading Down

To *trade up by trading down* is a sure way to get prospects to understand exactly what it is they want in the product you are selling. Any product has a good, better, and best version.

- Start your description with the very best product and a total explanation of what that product will do in terms of *features*, *advantages*, and *benefits*. We will refer to this method as the *FAB System*, which you'll learn more about in the next chapter.

- Move to the middle of the product line, and explain exactly what prospects will lose in FAB if they invest in this product.

- Next, drop to the low-end product and again show them all the FAB they will lose.

This approach will cause your prospects to move either to the middle- or top-of-the-line product.

Assign a Dollar Value to Every Feature

Every feature of your product has a dollar value that you must establish in your mind. You must first distinguish all the features between one product and the other. Make sure that you are able to convey the various features to the prospect, and use the phrasing "For a few dollars more you can have this feature."

SALES PRO TIP

Price Condition Early to Eliminate Surprise!
Price conditioning should start early in the presentation, even as early as the entry. The more times you price condition the prospects, the better they will understand the retail value that a product should sell for.

Price Conditioning

Price conditioning is also an extremely important process to establish product worth. Start price conditioning early in the presentation. Use terms such as "longer lasting," "brighter colors," "better manufacturing process." to give prospects some idea of the worth of the product.

Each time you price condition prospects, you establish a higher selling value for your product. This process is called *justifying the price*.

Another reason you must price condition early is to remove the preconceived price impression from prospects' minds as quickly as possible. All prospects have a preconceived notion of what a product should cost. And unfortunately, their expectation of price is usually a lot lower than the cost of a good product because so many companies hammer home low price points. They do this to draw phone calls into the company. And the technique isn't quite bait-and-switch advertising either, because the low-priced product usually is available. But the company does everything in its power not to sell it (and prospects should do everything in their power not to buy it). The trick the company uses is to have its sales representatives go out, create the trade-up-by-trading-down scenario, and walk away with an order somewhere in the middle, between their high- and low-priced products.

Remember that you have a product, just like everyone else does. Hopefully, your product is better than everyone else's product. You must present your product in a way that does it justice. You must make the product worth money to the prospects. Even so, if you lay the price on prospects all at one time, they will balk. You must present price in a way that each part of your product has a dollar value, and then keep building on those parts.

To price condition, justify your top-of-the-line product by adding a dollar value to each feature that it has over the middle-of-the-road product. If you don't do this, you will end up selling the mid-value product every time.

I think of selling the same as I do walking into a new-car showroom and visualizing the sticker price on an automobile. The price of the automobile is broken down, with the sticker listing everything you get for your expenditure, including dealer preparation and destination charges. Then, when you see the bottom line, you know what is included in that $40,000 or $50,000 sticker price.

Also remember that people in their right minds don't pay sticker price for an automobile. They will negotiate the price with the salesperson. But with the sticker price, they have access to the details that can give them some idea of where to start.

Using a picture portfolio to show your product and explain the cost is a good idea. You also can explain that "On other products, a small part could go bad, and that would keep a very expensive (quote the price of their product) from operating."

You must be cautious as you price condition. If the prospects start to challenge you about the price you've given for your product, calm them down and tell them you really have no idea yet what the actual price will be. You were just giving them some comparable product pricing.

At the same time, it's better to price condition high, so that when you do quote the price during the close, your prospects will be pleasantly surprised. Just remember: no matter what price you quote during the close, prospects will always say, "That's too much money." Whether the price is $5,000, $500, or $250, it will always be too much money.

Your prospects need to understand that two products might look alike and function quite similarly, yet one might be different from the other in many significant ways.

During interviews with people wishing employment at our company, I hand them a wristwatch and ask them to sell it to me. If they can't break the sales process down into little segments, explaining and putting a dollar value on each little piece of the watch to make it worth its weight in gold, they don't get the job.

Sales Without Profit—the Fool's Dream

You don't want to be a paperwork hero. If you have a great product, it might be time for you to realize that price does not sell a product. You must be well versed on presenting the **perception** of price to your prospects. It is up to you to give some type of price conditioning to prospects so they will feel that the value of the product far exceeds the selling price.

The problem arises, however, when you sell your product at a greatly reduced price. You can develop a false sense of security and actually begin to believe that you made money, when in actuality, after all the numbers are calculated, you discover that you have lost money.

Why would anyone want to sell a product and not make a dime? Sales organizations operate based on profit. Sales people quit because they don't receive commissions if they fail to make a profit for the company. Companies go out of business because they fail to make a profit.

Sales without profits are a fool's dream. Don't let yourself fall into this trap because you want to be a leader in sales at all costs—even if that means selling without a profit.

The Despite System

To convince prospects of product differences and sell your product, you must do something I like to call the *positive 8s* and avoid doing what I call the *negative 8s*. Your job is to **isolate** those product differences, along with any objections prospects might express. Have prospects **evaluate** how your product will save them money.

SALES PRO TIP

Stimulate, Don't Intimidate

Stimulate conversation, but never intimidate the prospect. If you make prospects feel intimidated, they will react with hostility toward you.

And when you disagree with prospects, you must disagree in such a way that you appear to be agreeing. Use "and" instead of "but" to achieve a stronger supportive connection while avoiding conflict. For example, you must learn to say, "I appreciate what you are saying and . . . ," or "I respect what you are saying and . . . ." Never challenge prospects in an attempt to win the battle, and end up losing the war.

Translate that savings into laymen's terms so prospects will see that this will be an investment in your product, not an expenditure. **Stimulate** the conversation with a positive attitude, and answer any questions. Have prospects **participate** when you **demonstrate** the product, to **educate** them about the differences between your product and everyone else's. When you successfully complete this process, it's up to the owner of your company to **compensate** you for a job well done.

Here are the *negative 8s* you must avoid doing with your prospects: Don't ever **irritate, intimidate, complicate, deviate, frustrate, incriminate, implicate,** or **obliterate** the sales presentation or the prospects.

Use Terms That Relate to Quality

I like to use statements such as "Long after the price is forgotten the quality of the goods lives on." or "Price buyers are twice buyers." Selling quality makes selling so much easier, because no one gets upset about owning the best. You must convey your product as the Cadillac of the products at Chevrolet prices.

But remember: none of this works if you really don't have a great product. You must believe in your product to use confidence selling. What prospects perceive is what prospects believe. You must do your job to help them understand the difference between your product and the others. And justify the price by assigning a dollar value to every item that is different between your product and the others.

Related to the idea of quality, I have incorporated in my lifestyle that when I shop for anything, I now just buy the best. I have had it with the bargain basement stuff that I used to bring home and found it didn't have all the features I thought it would have, so I ended up taking it back. Then I moved to the next one up in the line, watching my money so I didn't overspend, and ended up taking that one back and moving on to the next better one they had.

At this point, I don't care what it costs to get the best one. I have already spent sleepless nights, tons of gas, and lots of time packing and repackaging the goods, plus the time I spend on the highways driving back and forth between home and store.

To make a short story long, I now ask to see the top-of-the-line product, and I ask how much it costs. If I can't afford it, I don't buy it. I would rather wait until I can afford it, so I don't put myself through all that aggravation.

This is the same frustrating process that we put our prospects through when we ask them to settle for substandard merchandise.

Reduce to the Ridiculous

Break the prices you quote to prospects down to the miniscule. For instance, if your product costs $500 more than the other product, convey that difference as $50 a year for a 10-year period of time. Do you realize that amount is a little more than 13 cents a day?

Tell, Don't Sell

We have used the term *selling* throughout the opening sections of this book. But the confident salesperson is one who takes the word *sell* out of his vocabulary. People are sold a bill of goods every day. "Tell, not sell" is an important part of confidence selling. For example, if I were your best friend telling you about something that

SALES PRO TIP

Tell, Don't Sell
People don't like to feel as if they have been sold a bill of goods. They want to feel they were in control of what they purchased. It's our job to make them feel that way. We must be able to **tell** them our story without having to hard **sell**. If we tell them what our products can do, then it's up to them to make the right decision.

could literally save you thousands of dollars, would you consider that selling?

People are tired of being sold to by other people, family members, and even their children. As you know from personal experience, selling never stops, even if it's only your son or daughter trying to convince you why he or she should have a cell phone or the keys to your car.

And if you turn on the TV, you are hit with a barrage of advertisers trying to convince you that you should own their product. It's the same with the advertising on the radio, in movie theaters, and now even on the Internet, with the pop-ups designed to get your attention to "Place an order now!" Schools, churches, men, women, organizations—they all try to earn major dollars through sales.

Phone solicitation is another way people try to pique your interest in products. And try to find the news between all the sales advertisements in the newspaper. Magazines are no better, loaded with items to sell. You can't even read through your mail without having someone trying to sell you something using the United States Postal Service.

So you jump in your car to try to find comfort from people trying to sell you something, and you're hit in the face with a bombardment of advertisements on billboards, trucks, buses, and even taxi cabs.

Is there no end to the hand-written signs all over the telephone poles that say lose 30 pounds in 30 days or your money back, or if you own a computer, I can show you how to earn a $1,000 a day, working 5 hours a week.

I personally seek refuge in the church, to pray it all goes away. When I turn over the church bulletin, I tremble as I again see all the advertisements the parishioners have placed even there, to sell their products.

Now imagine, after all of this, you show up at the prospects' door to try and sell them something. You must be able to say to them about your product, "You make up your own mind what you want to do, and when you want to do it," or "You folks are old enough to make your own decision. Do what's in the best interest of you and your family."

All these approaches play an important role in confidence selling. Letting prospects have a say about what they want to do will bring about a better chance to write an order than if you bully your way through the presentation with high-pressure sales tactics. People can read through that kind of sales pitch, and they will be the first to let you know that they don't appreciate it. A no-nonsense sales approach makes more sense. People respect you when you respect them.

And even if prospects make an incorrect statement, it is wiser to say, "I appreciate what you're saying, and . . ." than to directly tell them they're wrong. Start to use this language, and I promise you will take the edge off the tendency to sell rather than tell.

Selling no longer takes on an argumentative approach. You are a guest in your prospects' house, so act like one. You must tone your statements so they don't offend.

Make Buying the Prospects' Idea

People don't buy from people they don't like. They can like you one minute, but the first time you raise the buying signal, they will bulk. Purchasing the product must be the prospects' idea. Telling

SALES PRO TIP

Never Lie
Don't say things you don't mean. If the prospects live in a rat hole, don't tell them they have a nice house. If their furniture is falling apart, don't compliment them on it. People can read through your line of bull. Dispose of the line of bull now, and promise yourself you will never use it again.

prospects all the ways your product can save them money, or time, or be of benefit to them can create the idea to buy in their minds. If they feel you've told them the truth, and they like what you've told them, it's a sale.

To "Tell, not sell" means you are honest at all times. If you're not an honest person to begin with, I suggest this be the day you make a pact never to lie again. If you need to lie about what your product will do, you shouldn't be selling it. (That is, of course, unless you're just a crook and want to swindle people out of their life savings and worthy possessions. In that case, put down this book; it's not for you).

We still have salespeople out there using the Flip Wilson theory, "A lie is as good as the truth, if you can get someone to believe it." But we must be trustworthy people who want to make an honest buck, selling an honest product, promoted by an honest company, buying from an honest manufacturer, who buys its material from honest suppliers.

The hardest lesson for a salesperson to learn is that if you lie, it will always come back to haunt you. If you lie, then you have to tell other lies to address the lie you were caught in, and it become a vicious, never-ending cycle.

Some people call lying *puffery*, which is supposedly an OK method of lying to prospects and getting away with it. But the best way to deal with any situation is don't lie. You're better off losing a sale than losing sleep worrying over something you said that was a mis-truth. It's easier to deal with the situation honestly while you are face to face with prospects, and address their concerns rather than try to bluff your way around the concerns and lie.

Gain Trust by Earning Trust

The simplest way to gain trust is to earn trust. You earn trust by being trustworthy. We all are creatures of habit. You have the right to formulate good habits or bad habits. I pride myself on formulating good habits, but I haven't always been that way. I can't sit here and tell you that I was not on the other end of the spectrum. I have been there, and done that, and I have the tee shirt to prove it.

I try to bring about respect in my life now, and I don't lie. I will never go back from whence I came, and my life is much simpler now.

So we are back to "Tell, don't sell." Tell about a product that is worth its weight in gold, and you have something to say. Again, your product must have all the right bells and whistles to be a viable product to talk about. If the product won't perform, can't perform, and isn't worth the money required to produce it, you will have to sell rather than tell—you will have to lie—to your prospects.

When you have spent enough time on the warm up to know the prospects are listening to you, you're ready to start creating need for your product.

Create Need

- Paint Pictures with Words

- Discuss Features, Advantages, and Benefits

- Gather Information

- Justify Price

- Get Prospects Used to Saying Yes

- Defer Objections; Plan How and When to Overcome

- Listen Carefully

- Create Urgency

- Think on Your Feet

- Eliminate Competition

- Analyze Selling Situation

STEP 3

Create Need

STEP 1
Entry

STEP 2
Warm-up

STEP 3
Create Need
Discover Problems
Promise Solutions
Discuss Benefits

STEP 4
Company Story

STEP 5
Kill Options

STEP 6
Product Presentation

STEP 7
Pre-Close

STEP 8
Close

STEP 9
Post Close

STEP 10
Replace the Lead

People buy when they want, or believe they need, the product you are selling. They buy things that make their life easier and more comfortable. It's your job to create the desire and the need for the prospects to invest in your product. The secret to creating these emotions is to make your presentation compelling, to show how your product can fulfill the prospects' wants and needs.

Paint Word Pictures

Painting pictures with words is easier than it sounds. Let's say I want to describe domestic float glass used in the window business. Here's an example of how I might paint with words:

> Picture this if you will. The glassmakers take glass in a molten state, pour it onto a lead base, and then let it come to rest like a still pond. Picture a still pond—no imperfections; you don't see a ripple, just a smooth, flat surface. Then they

---

CREATE means

        Communicate with prospects.

        Reinforce prospects' statements.

        Eliminate competition.

        Analyze the selling situation.

        Tell your story.

        Elicit information.

Through communication, you will reinforce statements prospects make, eliminate competition, and constantly analyze the selling situation. And you must continue to tell your story and elicit information all the way through the close.

---

skim that smooth, flat surface to remove floating debris, and you have the perfect piece of glass.

Sequential Selling

Explaining things in sequence helps to tell the story in a way prospects can easily follow. Explaining in sequence is called a *geared selling presentation*. Use your own creativity to flow the presentation sequentially and stay within the confines of an organized sales plan that is not a canned presentation.

SALES PRO TIP

To Sell the Lead, Create a Need
People don't normally purchase things they don't need. Sometimes prospects don't understand that they genuinely have a need for your product. So it is up to you to create that need.

Prospects rely on you to have the right answers at the right time. You must also justify the price so prospects understand exactly why they want and need your product. You must build urgency and credibility so you can close the deal and maintain customer satisfaction.

The FAB System

To create need, you must ask a three-part questi
the *FAB (features, advantages, and benefits) Sy.*

1. "What do you like about the product you are currently using?"
2. "What do you dislike about the product you are currently using?"
3. "If you were ever going to change the product you are currently using, what would you change about it?"

Apply this information to the sales presentation by telling the prospects about all the product's *features*. Explain that, from every product feature, prospects will derive a definite *advantage*. However, they will be more interested in understanding the *benefits* that you attribute to this product.

You can assign the FAB system to anything you want. I like to use the example of a Styrofoam cup. Think of all the features of the Styrofoam cup. You could probably find 100 features, advantages, and benefits for a Styrofoam cup. Here are a few:

Feature: It's made of Styrofoam.

Advantage: Because it's Styrofoam, the cup will not burn your hand if you put something hot into it.

Benefit: You can hold the cup while it's hot, which keeps you from dropping it or spilling the hot liquid on your clothes. This saves you money on dry cleaning or replacing your good clothes, which probably cost you hundreds of dollars to purchase.

The *features* component is something good about the product: what it's made of; its shape; its color; that it can be stacked, is disposable, has a lip around the top edge, and can keep things hot or cold for a long time. Each feature mentioned has an *advantage,* such as durability, comfortable to hold, efficient, etc.

But what your prospects are truly interested in are the *benefits* they will derive from these advantages. And these product benefits must be significant to prospects: how the product will save them time

---

SALES PRO TIP

Telegraph, Don't Write Letters
The best telegram in the world can deliver an important message in 12 words or less. Remember that when you tell prospects about your product. Limit your words to the essential features, advantages, and benefits. In other words, telegraph, don't write letters.

---

and money, for example. If you cannot demonstrate a product's benefits to your prospects, you can forget telling them anything else about it because they won't be convinced enough to buy.

Offer What They Want—Now

You must have all buying parties present when you are creating need for your product. Then you begin to do whatever it is that you do to create the need. Whether you start to analyze, measure, or review what the prospects currently have, your goal is to talk about the problems you see with the product they are using now. This is the only way you can elaborate on the differences and the benefits they will derive from investing in your product over the other product they are currently using.

To create need, you must also create some sense of urgency within your prospects. One way to do this is to find out how your product will save them money. Then you must ask this question: "If you were ever going to start saving money, when do you think the right time would be to start?" I'm sure the answer would be Now.

SALES PRO TIP

Keep Perspective
Always remember that the prospects did not wake up this morning and say, "Today is the day I think I will buy your product."

Justify the Price

If yours is a new product, or something prospects don't already own, then you need to create need for the product in terms of how it will benefit them. Let's assume the product is a water softener, or an electronic air filter, or a central vacuum cleaner. You must stimulate the conversation by showing the prospects what this device will do for them in terms of benefits. And the bottom line— what people are really interested in—is how the product will save them time and money.

He Who Knows the Most Controls the Selling Situation

I recently made a trip to Atlantic City, and while I was in Caesars Palace, I visited a fine men's shop called Oggi. My wife, my 15-year-old son, and I were browsing the sweater department when a salesman named Jerry Krumaker approached us. He was an excellent sales person—not pushy, definitely a confident sales person. Remember, Jerry knew his stuff and had the control, based on his vast knowledge of the clothing industry.

When I asked him about Coogi Sweaters, a top-of-the-line sweater that sells for about $385, he proceeded to tell me that Coogi recently went out of business. He said it was a shame because Coogi manufactured top-quality merchandise. Jerry said he had met the owner of Coogi, and that he was a great guy and took a vested interest in the merchandising of his product. Jerry went on to explain how no two Coogi sweaters are exactly alike, and that their durability is next to none. Jerry explained how they are made, and that the sewing machines control 18 colors of thread. Coogi even attaches a tool for mending the thread pulls—which the company assures you will happen, but it gives you a way to repair the thread pulls easily.

Jerry showed me some other sweaters that have tried to emulate Coogi. (Notice: Emulation is the greatest form of flattery.) Remember, he didn't even have a Coogi to sell, but he made me grateful for the one I purchased from another store a month earlier.

Now here comes the beauty of this story. My 15-year-old son, who works at Subway sandwich shop, looked up at me after we had left the store and said, "As soon as we get home, I'm using my paycheck to buy a Coogi sweater. I have to have it!" You see, Jerry did a great job selling Coogi, and he justified the price so well that even a 15-year-old understood its value and was sold on the idea of owning one.

I will return to Oggi and visit Jerry, and I will buy whatever he suggests I buy.

Remember also that you must get a commitment from prospects that your product is far superior to whatever they have seen before. You must ask this question: "If you were ever going to invest in this kind of product, would this be the product you would invest in?" With this commitment, you price condition the prospect.

Creating need also takes into account all the bad things that could happen if the prospects do not purchase the product. Bad is good when it comes to creating need. For instance, when I talk about windows, I say:

> Mr. and Mrs. Prospect, you have a large amount of condensation coming through that single pane of glass. Understand that heat seeks cold, and you have what we call in the business 'through-to-through conductivity,' or transfer of cold air to meet warm air masses, which forms condensation.
>
> Let's say you put ice into a glass, and then fill the glass with water. The next thing you know, you need a coaster to catch the water that forms on the outside of the glass, to keep the water from ruining your table. The same thing is happening with your windows.
>
> I really don't care about the moisture on the window, but I do care about where the water is going from there. Right now, it is seeping down the window and into the wood, causing dry rot and sill deterioration. You know what happens to moisture-ridden wood? It becomes bug infested. And if you think we are expensive, hire an exterminator. And you will also need a drywall person to rip off the drywall, and a carpenter to replace the deteriorated studs. Hopefully, you have some of this wallpaper left, because you're going to need it, too. Or maybe you should just consider doing the whole room with new wallpaper or paint, because even if the wallpaper were available, it would be from a different dye lot. You also will probably need an electrician, because the electric outlet right underneath the window, where the water is currently running down, will probably be damaged. In the meantime, be careful because that situation might start a fire. You know, water and electricity don't mix.

I think you get the idea. Bad is good. Nothing I said in the above statement is incorrect. And I painted clear pictures for the prospects in terms of what might happen if they don't invest in my product.

SALES PRO TIP

He Who Knows the Most Controls the Selling Situation.
Remember that controlling the selling situation is just a matter of knowing your product and knowing your competition. It's up to you to do the research on your competition, and to know the companies and their products inside and out.

Eliciting Information

Now it's time to elicit information that you will use later on in the selling presentation. One question you might want to ask prospects is "How soon do you think it will be before you will be making a decision about investing in this product?"

Now let's say they respond, "Oh, in about a year."

You then say, "That soon."

Let's say they answer, "In about two years."

Your response will be "That soon." No matter what they say, your response will be "That soon." You follow this response with "I didn't know you wanted to get started on it that quickly."

Postponement is the easiest prospect resistance to overcome. You can plot the future for them:

> Mr. and Mrs. Prospect, two things happen for those who wait. One, the price continues to go up, and two, you still have the same problems you have today. Let's just take a look at what you have, I'll show you what I have, and then you make the decision. How does that sound to you, Mr. And Mrs. Prospect? Fair enough?

You can always sell time delays for payment, with either monthly installments or deferred payment plans. To be successful with this approach, you must get the prospects to agree: "It's cheaper to absorb the interest rate now than experience the cost-of-living escalation if we wait and buy later."

Reinforcement and Feedback

You are in the process of using a sales philosophy I call reinforcement and feedback. Briefly, the process involves storing what prospects say, reinforcing their thoughts later on in the sales presentation, and then feeding the information back to them. At that point, it becomes their idea.

For instance, you might say to prospects:

> Remember early on, when you said you wanted a product to be able to do this, that, and the other? [I just reinforced what the prospects said. Now I need to feed it back to them.] Well, I have great news for you; our product is one of the very few products that will do everything you want it to do—this, that, and the other. [I just used feedback, feeding the prospects' own words right back to them.]

The prospects told me exactly what they wanted. I reinforced the fact that what they wanted was a great idea, and I explained through feedback that my product had everything they were looking for.

Prospects Tell You How to Close

Throughout this process, you must keep the conversation flowing, and you must listen to the prospects very closely. If you listen, they will tell you how to close them. If they tell you what they want in a product, rather than coming right out and saying, "Our product has that!" say instead, "So Mr. and Mrs. Prospect, when it comes time to invest in this kind of product, you definitely would want it to have that feature or you wouldn't consider investing in it. Is that correct?" Remember, get them to say Yes and keep them saying Yes.

Next ask, "What other features would you consider important in an investment of this magnitude?"

Now they will have to elaborate on exactly what they are looking for when it comes time for them to select a product. This is a good time to make mental notes and prepare for the reinforcement and feedback, which you will use later.

Create, But Don't Deviate

When you are in front of prospects, you are on stage. You will be paid based on your performance. When you become creative, make sure you stay within the confines of the sales plan.

Most good sale people have the ability to ad lib and become super-creative. These are the golden moments when you are truly on; you feel up and are on a natural high. At such times, you can get great vibes from prospects, and you can intuit them. When you feel this way, it's easy to go off on a tangent and deviate from the sales plan. Instead, use the geared presentation to create the selling situation you want, but don't deviate from the plan.

Be creative when you work the sales plan. You must have the ability to think on your feet in every potential selling situation. Consider the following story.

In a small town, a gentleman walked into a bank and asked to speak to the manager. The manager came out, introduced himself, and asked how he could be of assistance. The man said he would like to borrow $5,000. The banker asked if he was a local, and the man said no, he was from New York. The banker told him he could not arrange the loan. The man said, "Look. I have a 2002 Rolls Royce outside, and here are the title and keys. All I need is $5,000 for one week, and then I'll be back to pick up my car and title." The banker took the keys and title, and gave the man $5,000 cash.

When the man left, the banker ran a credit check on him and found out that he was a multibillionaire. The banker became confused about why the man had asked for a paltry $5,000. One week later, the man came back and asked to see the banker. He gave the banker $5,000 in cash, said if he had figured correctly he also owed $35 interest (which he gave him), and asked for his title and keys back.

The banker gave them to him, and he asked the man why he had done what he did. He told him he knew he was a billionaire and

could borrow any sum of money he would like at any lending institution he might choose. The man said, "Good lord, man! I didn't
need the money! You tell me where else I could safely park my Rolls
in this town and have somebody watch it for one week as if it were
his own, for a mere $35?"

That's thinking on your feet. So be creative when you are with
potential clients.

Company Story

- Create Trust

- Establish Company Reputation

- Use Testimonials and Portfolios

- Mention Membership of Professional Organizations

- Set the Pace

- Sell the Best, Forget the Rest

STEP 4

Company Story

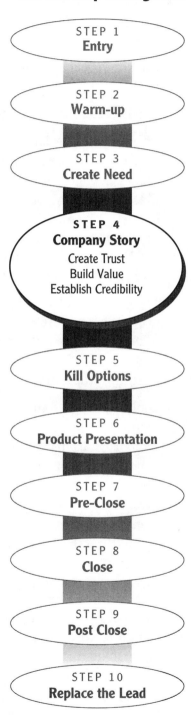

The Ten Step Selling Plan

STEP 1
Entry

STEP 2
Warm-up

STEP 3
Create Need

STEP 4
Company Story
Create Trust
Build Value
Establish Credibility

STEP 5
Kill Options

STEP 6
Product Presentation

STEP 7
Pre-Close

STEP 8
Close

STEP 9
Post Close

STEP 10
Replace the Lead

A major step in the 10-step selling plan is the company story. To talk a great company story, you must work for a great company.

The major mark of a great company is its history and reputation. People love companies that have been in business a long time—and they buy products from such companies.

Name Recognition

If you stop to think about it, one major reason prospects choose a company is name recognition. Companies invest lots of money to develop name recognition. Every day we see company names plastered all over billboards, on company trucks, and in print. If you notice this kind of advertising, you will also notice that the price of the company's product generally doesn't appear.

You can easily "brand" names on many products that are out there. If

I say name an expensive watch, you might say Rolex. If I say name a great shirt, you might say Polo or Nautica. If I say name a high-end car, you might say Porsche, Mercedes, or BMW.

These companies have spent tons of cash just to get name recognition because they know how important it is.

I have never heard anybody say anything bad about H.J. Heinz. I have heard people say they love Heinz ketchup and other Heinz products. Major companies that have longevity, such as General Electric, Westinghouse, Phillips, Carrier, Black & Decker, Sears, Hewlett Packard, Ford, Canon, Apple, and so many others, have many good things going for them. They are financially responsible, and they have a number of employees and assets; but beyond all, they have name recognition.

To be successful selling your product, the company you work for needs the same things going for it, although its name recognition might be on a smaller scale than the most well-known companies. When people shop, they first go for the brand-name products, at least until they find out how much they cost.

Look at the youth today and judge for yourself how important brand names can be. Many kids are all wrapped up in the status symbol syndrome companies and their advertising agencies have created. What some young people pay for one shirt or sweater, I could have spent to buy a three-piece suit just 10 years back. Some parents even buy tennis shoes on monthly payments for their children. For many young people, wearing off-brand clothes is equal to committing the proverbial mortal sin.

Customer Service: Key to Word-of-Mouth Advertising

How does a company product become a brand-name product? The answer is word-of-mouth advertising. You as a consumer must understand that good news travels fast, and bad news travels faster. That means when a company sells a great product, people will tell other people, and it won't be long before the company has established great name recognition.

Now let's talk about the bad news. If the same consumers who tell their friends about a product they like have a bad experience with your product and company, they will tell at least 3 other people. And each of those 3 people, who have never even used your product, much less know about your company, will tell 3 other people. Now 12 people have formulated an opinion about your product and company without meeting you or seeing your product. And believe me, it doesn't stop there. Negative feedback about a product or company is a never-ending process that ultimately leads many products and companies to bankruptcy.

That's why, for example, I'm so emphatic about our company servicing our prospects. For the year 2002—on the radio show I have hosted for the past two and a half years, called *Your Home, Your Views*, on WCBM 680—I made a commitment to satisfy 100 percent of the people 100 percent of the time.

To do this, my goal has been to incorporate everyone in our entire company to become "service aware." Our goal is to become 100 percent service oriented, and that starts with products that are virtually service free or easy to repair.

The main problem we have had reaching this goal relates to our customers, who sometimes don't seem to cooperate. Let me explain. Customers are so used to dealing with fly-by-night organizations, or with people who are not on the same wavelength as we are that they become skeptical. They doubt our willingness to do anything and everything to resolve a complaint. For a company to behave as we do is not normal to them, even though more good companies today have policies similar to ours. Many prospects have become so accustomed to disrespectful treatment by businesses that they keep their guard up.

The sad part is, if customers have a problem with our product, we are often the last to know. The customers have already discussed the problem with friends, neighbors, and business associates, and those people add fuel to the fire by relaying information to our customers about all the problems they have encountered with other companies. Fueled by this input, our customers make their next call to the consumer protection agencies, and then we finally receive a letter stating we have 10 days to resolve the complaint—which we probably could have handled the next day if our customers had contacted us immediately.

A key question to ask yourself is "Who do I really work for?" Allow me to answer that: the customer. Customers will make you or break you. They control how much money you will make. Therefore, it's up to you to keep them happy.

The Question Is Not When, But with Whom

Always remember that when prospects postpone a buying decision because they want to shop around, it's probably time for you to get some clarification. Prospects are afraid to commit for a reason. They might say, "We never make a quick decision," or "We don't do anything unless we sleep on it."

But I always ask, "Why is that? Is it because you have been stung before?"

They often answer, "*Yes*, as a matter of fact, we have."

Then I respond, "Mr. and Mrs. Prospect, it's not a question of when you deal, but with whom." You can make this response if you work for a great company.

As a salesperson, you will be dealing with only two things: a product and a company. You could have the greatest company in the world, but if you make a shoddy product, you have nothing. By the same token, you could have a great product, but if the company is financially flushed and unable to distribute that product, again you have nothing.

Highlight to prospects all the good things about your company. For example, talk about all the organizations your company belongs to and all the great things your company has done.

Your prospects must agree on two things about your company. The first question you must ask is "If you ever were going to do business with someone, does my company sound like the type of company you would want to do business with?" Prospects must answer this question *Yes*.

Your next question will be "Why?" You need to hear them justify why they would want to deal with your company very clearly over any other company out there.

Another question you will ask later is "If you were ever going to buy a product, does this look like the product you would want?" Again you want their answer to be *Yes*.

And then again you will ask, "Why?"

Sell the Best, Forget the Rest

To sell successfully, you must have the finest product on the market. You must have total belief in your product, a belief from which you can truthfully say you personally would own it. And if you do own the product, that's even better. If you have this passion for your product, you are on the right track.

Some salespeople think they can push any product. The problem is that with an inferior product, you must lie about what it can do and how well it will perform. And you know bad news travels fast, so it won't be long before your prospects find out and spread the word about what you sold them.

Save yourself this time and trouble, and look for the best product to sell, even if it costs more. Keep out of the flim-flam sales game—it gets old real quick. You don't want to always be looking over your shoulder and having to answer calls from angry customers who have lost all respect for you.

Service to Sell

I take service very seriously, just as any good company does. I'm in this business for the long haul, and I will continue to think of ways in which we can better handle incoming service calls.

Too many times, products fail when our office is closed. When people go to bed knowing about a pending service problem, and they're unable to take any action about it until the next business day, they have all night or even all weekend to think about all the bad things that might happen—and to formulate bad opinions of our product and our company. Then they take our number to work, where they forget or get too busy to call, and the problem can continue for some time.

To prevent this scenario, we have a link on our website through which people can report problems and request service calls. We tell our customers to go to the service page there, which is available 24 hours a day, seven days a week. They can report their service need and leave the phone number where they can be reached. We will call them the next day to schedule the service. Visit homeviewinc.com or Homeview.ws to take a look at our setup for this process.

Companies need to place even more emphasis on service than on selling the product itself. If your company sells a product that might require service, you must be able to boast about your great service department.

And as a salesperson, make service a part of your company's daily ritual, whether at your sales meetings, regional meetings, or board meetings. The first question that should come up at these meetings is "Are we having any service-related problems?" Make every person your company employs—your administrator, your sales secretary, and any support personnel—a customer service representative. Every person in the entire organization should have the ability and

SALES PRO TIP

The Speed of the Leader Is the Speed of the Team
If you are in any kind of management position, you must set the pace for the rest of your sales people. Make it your practice to be the leader in the sales field.

out of business; it's just something that happens when the amount of money going out exceeds the amount of money coming in. I think the government calls it deficit spending. The ultimate plan of new companies—the American Dream—is not to file Chapter 7, 11, or 13 or fall by the wayside.

Some of the things people look for in a great company are that it is financially responsible, it has a number of employees, and it has assets. So many times people judge good companies as those that have a tremendous amount of overhead. But a company with tremendous overhead won't be in business very long.

A great business must be financially solvent. It must be able to meet payroll, its rent or mortgage payment, its manufacturing bills, its phone bills, its heat and light bills, and its insurance premiums. And it must be able to do all this without worrying about where the next dollar is coming from.

A great company doesn't need your money to function. It can meet payroll without its salespeople remunerating a dime to it. Please don't misunderstand me in reference to this statement. Companies are entitled to one-third down from customers on custom-made products, and the balance on satisfactory completion of the job or when the product is delivered.

Use Picture Portfolios and Testimonial Letters

Most salespeople are in a real bind when it comes to establishing credibility for their company if it has been in business only a short time. How does one justify being in business for a month? Often, salespeople lie and over-exaggerate how long the company has been around. Fortunately for honest companies and salespeople, the consumer has the wherewithal to check the longevity of any company through consumer organizations such as the Better Business Bureau (BBB) or Dunn & Bradstreet (D&B).

The best ways to justify your company are to use a picture portfolio to show your product in use, and to carry testimonial letters from previous customers who are satisfied with your product. (And remember that to get testimonial letters, you must ask for them.)

The more credentials you have, the more credibility you have, the more you can justify your company, and the better off you are. As an example, because our company, Homeview Contractors Inc., is in the home improvement and remodeling business, we explain our insurance, which is very important in our industry. We show proof of insurance—Workers' Compensation, public liability—and that we are bonded. We also show our membership in the Better Business Bureau, National Association for the Remodeling Industry (NARI), Maryland Home Improvement Commission (MHIC), and Maryland Improvement Council Association (MICA). We tell people that this is how intelligent consumers shop. They make sure the company is legitimate. And the chances are 9 out of 10 that serious prospects will tell you they have already checked you out anyway.

Highlight Out-of-Business Companies in Yellow Pages

As part of giving my company story to prospects, I like to show them a marked-up copy of the local phone book yellow pages. I regularly go to the yellow pages and find the section that has the product I sell. Then I call all the listings to see whether they are still in business. I then photocopy these pages and highlight in yellow all the companies that have gone by the wayside or belly up.

Then when I meet with the prospects, I tell them:

> Let me show you my own form of yellow pages. See all the companies highlighted in yellow? They are now defunct, no longer in business. If you call, you'll get a recording saying, "I'm sorry, the number you have reached is no longer in service. Make sure you are dialing the right number. If you need assistance, stay on the line and an operator will be with you." Now I ask you, what is the operator going to do, service your broken product?

You want to incorporate in your sales presentation that if prospects don't deal with you, they need to deal with a company like yours. What are you saying to prospects when you say this? You are issuing them a challenge to find a company on the same wavelength as your company. You must feel that finding another similar company will be pretty hard for them to do, or else you probably won't want to issue the challenge. This is the kind of confidence selling you should be doing at all times.

Enthusiasm Sells

As for you, the first essential ingredient for successful selling is enthusiasm. It's that spirit of ambition that springs from within. It's the belief in your company and its products. You must have this belief. Without it, you will lose that mental energy that drives a person to think and work. Love of your company and product will give you enthusiasm. Knowledge of your company and product will build enthusiasm.

Once again, you must understand that to sell your product, you must sell the company. And the only security prospects have from any company selling a product they would invest in comes from honesty, reliability, integrity, and a guarantee. Therefore, it is up to you to convince your prospects that they will derive all these benefits when they deal with your company.

Explain How to Pay

You must also set up for prospects how they can pay for your product or service. Many prospects that you talk with will tell you up front that they will be paying cash. Most people are cash buyers until they hear the price. After that, unless you give them other reasonable options, they will be only strangers because you probably will never see them again.

You must establish up front that your company has two ways for prospects to pay for a product: "One is cash, if your name is Rockefeller or Tiger Woods." You want to clarify that so they know the product is going to be expensive.

> The second option is a convenient, monthly payment plan we arrange through a reputable lending institution. Remember, Mr. and Mrs. Prospect, it's cheaper now to absorb the interest rate than it is the cost-of-living escalation, which will make the product much more expensive if you buy it later.

You must ensure that your company is dealing with a reputable lending institution, not somebody like Fred's Bank. You might want to say something like:

> Mr. and Mrs. Prospect, we have the ability to arrange the financing here in the convenience of your own home, without your running to the bank. We probably can get a much better interest rate because of our long relationship with this bank. You see, this bank will bend over backward to please us.

Taking this approach builds tremendous credibility with prospects, when they know the bank lets you write its paperwork in their home.

This tactic also helps to keep your prospects from going to their credit union to get money to purchase the product, where too often someone who knows nothing about your product tells them they are spending too much money. In that case, the end result is likely to be a sales cancellation because the prospects are still going through buyer's remorse, which we will discuss later at great length.

Discounting the Price

When you are discussing your company, you also want to set up early in prospects' minds that you want their business, you need their business, and you will do anything to get their business, even if that means discounting a price. You always want to leave that option open and plant the seed early, so prospects understand that they have some room to negotiate—as they should. I don't know about you, but nobody I know wants to pay retail prices.

And when you start discount pricing, make sure prospects understand that the discount is coming out of your pocket, not out of the company. I always say, point blank:

> You see Mr. and Mrs. Prospect, the company will still make its profit. That's why it's in business, and the profit is what keeps it in business. So please understand that I can't discount into the company's profit margin.

People respect and understand that companies are in business to make money. By making this statement, you are bringing truth and credibility to the table and to the presentation. (And it had better be the truth. No company is in business to trade dollars, or worse, lose money.) Furthermore, by building on all of your company's positive attributes, you strengthen your position with the prospects. And anything you can do to stabilize the selling situation will benefit you greatly when you zero in on the close.

Deal from Strength, Not Weakness

One of the hardest lessons you will ever learn in sales is to always deal from strength and never from weakness. Operating from a position of strength is a hard goal to achieve, and to do so consistently might take you some time.

You must first accept the fact that, as human beings, we often let our feelings control our thought processes, which is completely backward from how we need to function as salespeople. Think about it: how many times have you let your feelings control the way you think? Instead, your thought processes—how you think—must control your feelings. You must always deal from strength when you work with prospects. Remember: "Nothing a prospect will say or do will discourage me from making a complete and thorough presentation."

The purpose of the company story phase of the selling plan is to give you insight into how good companies are run, and how you can promote your company and your product to prospects. With this information in hand, you will be able to converse at length about your company—and differentiate it from every other company out there.

STEP 5

Kill Options

- Prospects Have Options; Cover all Options

- Price Condition

- Have Prospect Make Mini Decisions

- Don't Knock Your Competition

- Know Your Competition

- Control the Selling Situation

- Sell Your Product to the Exclusion of all Others

- Not Only Is Your Product the Right Choice,
  It's the Only Choice

- Use Word Target Responses

STEP 5

Kill Options

The Ten Step Selling Plan

STEP 1
Entry

STEP 2
Warm-up

STEP 3
Create Need

STEP 4
Company Story

STEP 5
Kill Options
Cover All Options
Price Condition

STEP 6
Product Presentation

STEP 7
Pre-Close

STEP 8
Close

STEP 9
Post Close

STEP 10
Replace the Lead

When you think about it, prospects have a number of different options when it comes to replacement products or new products that might be of some benefit to them. The primary purpose behind killing prospect options is to narrow the selection of products prospects might want to see. Your goal is to eliminate alternatives.

Mini-Decisions Stimulate Major Decisions

For a sale, prospects must make a series of mini-decisions. You must be able to reinforce these decisions appropriately so they will make the ultimate major decision to buy your product.

Before we go further, let's clarify what a decision is. A decision is a course of behavior chosen from a number of possible alternatives. The decision-making process is what is

67

going on in prospects' minds as you continue your journey through price conditioning and trying to eliminate competition.

The first option that prospects have, the first decision they might make, is to do absolutely nothing. As hard as this is to imagine, they do have that option. Your job as a sales representative is to discourage them from making that decision. As we discussed earlier, prospects also might tell you that "We never make a decision on the first night." If they say this, you can say nicely:

> You see, Mr. and Mrs. Prospect, you in fact already *have* made a decision—exactly what you said you wouldn't do, by deciding not to make a decision on the first night. I respect what you're saying; however, let me share with you some success stories of people just like yourself.

Feel, Felt, Found

At this point, you can go on to use something called "Feel, felt, found." Let's say the prospects' objection is "That's a lot of money!" Then you say:

> You know Mr. and Mrs. Prospect, I'm glad you said that because I know exactly how you **feel**. Many of my clients who have invested in our product in the past have **felt** exactly as you do. But after they used our product, let me tell you what they **found**. They found that they had saved a tremendous amount of money, enough to pay for the product in just a few years. They also found that with our product they saved in other places as well, which more than compensated them for the initial

SALES PRO TIP

Use Feel, Felt, Found

To present evidence to prospects based on the experiences of other satisfied customers, let prospects know you understand how they **feel**, that other clients have **felt** similarly, and after they bought the product, they **found** it to be everything they expected, and even more.

outlay of cash. And to this day my product continues to yield my clients a profit. They are so happy they made the investment!

Let's try this approach one more time with a different objection: "I really like what I see, but I don't think I can afford it right now." You respond:

> Mr. And Mrs. Prospect, I know exactly how you **feel**. Many clients who I have shown our product to **felt** exactly as you do, wanting to wait because they didn't think they could afford it. But after using our product, they **found** that they couldn't afford not to have it. It actually paid for itself within two years and than went on to save them thousands of dollars. You too will experience the same thing. I guess what I'm asking for is 10 percent of your trust, and I will earn the other 90 percent. What do you say?

Don't Knock Your Competition

Once again, as you are killing options for prospects, it's vital that you do so with kid gloves. In particular, do not slam other companies. I emphasized this earlier, but the point is worth repeating. There is a right way and a wrong way to discourage people from dealing with other companies, and neither involves conversation about the financial liquidity of the company or using hearsay information about whether or not the company services its prospects.

If I do have first-hand information that a company does not service its customers, I will advise prospects to make sure they check out information about the company before they enter into any financial transactions with it. To do this, they will need to use third-party information, such as they might get from the Better Business Bureau, about the company's track record for how it treats customers and responds to their complaints.

I will also ask the prospects to check out our company while they have the Protection Agency or other third-party agency on the phone. This approach builds instant credibility with your prospects. At the same time, you are not the one delivering the destructive information about the other company.

Third-Party Influence Sells

You must become acquainted with using third-party influence in every selling situation. Third-party influence means that prospects can be influenced in their decisions about whether to invest in your product by information from a third party. Third-party influence might come from friends or relatives of the prospects, another company with whom they do business, competitors' representatives, or printed material about your product or your competitors' products. You must be able to use third-party influence in support of your product. You also must be able to counter third-party influence that prospects are exposed to that might discourage them from buying your product.

When you are trying to bring home a point, having third-party influence about your product available to back you up is priceless. This third-party influence usually comes from magazines, newspaper articles, or anything that is in print from credible and reliable sources, and preferably from well-known people or publications. And if you are using vital statistics, it helps if you memorize the information and let your prospects read it directly from the magazine or other printed source.

Be Smart, Tear It Apart

When you present your product, you need to be prepared to break it down completely and sell prospects on all its features and benefits. And if you are going to compare your product with other products, you should have those products at your disposal. You want to be able to show the differences by letting prospects feel your product and the competitive product simultaneously.

Let prospects formulate their own opinions about the products, and let them voice those opinions. Remember that, as long as it's true, you can do this with the proviso that your product is, for example, heavier and better than the competition. But if it's not, this is a simple problem to overcome.

If the competition has a heavier, better product than yours, just go to work for the competition. Problem solved. I mean this sincerely—that you have a great product is of the utmost importance. You must feel confident that your product is the finest product on the market today. You can project this inner feeling to the prospect, and your product becomes that much easier to sell.

Research, Research, Research

You've probably heard the old adage that the product can sell itself. Bad news, partner—it can't. The product doesn't have a mouth with which to speak or a brain with which to present itself to the prospect. That's where you come in and why you are employed.

This brings us to the next requirement. You must know your competition, and know them well, which involves doing a lot of research. There is no such thing as too much research, and you can definitely do too little. Again, "He who knows the most controls the selling situation." (And if you want to find excuses why you can't research your competition, remember: "Excuses satisfy only those who make them!")

One of the most important things you can do is strive to learn one thing new every day, whether that's a new way to promote your product, or a new statement to include in your product presentation. To sell your product to the exclusion of all other products, you must know how to kill options without killing your presentation. If you've done your research, you will have the weapons in hand to do this.

Price Buyers Are Twice Buyers

Every product on the market today has a good, better, and best version. Some companies offer inexpensive products, less expensive products, and low-end products they sell for minimum cost. The sad part is, people often buy these worthless products because they're cheap.

The point that you need to get across to prospects is that they'll be making a decision about whether they want to do it right when they purchase a product, or whether they want to do it twice. You must clearly impress upon them what I've referred to a couple of times earlier in the book: "Price buyers are twice buyers."

Disposable or Permanent?

I like to classify the junk on the market as being disposable product, similar to a disposable lighter. It feels cheap, it's made cheap, it looks cheap, and it's cheap to buy. You'll want to emphasize to your prospects that they can buy two different types of product—one is disposable, and the other is permanent. To further clarify, you must ask prospects:

> Mr. and Mrs. Prospect, if you were ever going to make a change or purchase a product, would you want to make it a permanent change? Or would you rather go the less expensive way and consider repurchasing or replacing the product again sometime in the future?"

This is where the disposable and permanent products come into play.

> Mr. and Mrs. Prospect, there are two ways to this, a right way and a wrong way. Are you looking for a permanent solution to the problems you now encounter, or do you want to put a Band-Aid over a wound that requires a tourniquet?

Statements like these might bring out strong reaction from the prospects. Once again, you are using words to paint pictures, which you'll want to do throughout the entire presentation.

The Right and Only Choice!

Remember that each and every product is made from some kind of material. You should know everything there is to know about this material. If the product is for outdoor use, will it hold up in inclement weather? Is the product something that requires continual maintenance, or will it maintain its beauty for years to come?

All these details are important when you start talking alternatives with prospects. You must be able to convince them beyond any shadow of a doubt that your product is not only the right choice, but it's also the only choice.

Because I sell windows, let's consider them as a product. What type of material are windows made from? Wood, vinyl, aluminum, steel, and fiberglass. Each of these materials has strengths and weaknesses.

Wood is the greatest insulator known to man. You can set the end of a foot-long stick on fire, and you can't feel the heat transfer from the burning portion to the end you are holding. Unfortunately, wood has a major drawback. It expands and contracts in changing weather climates, and at the wrong time. In winter, the wood contracts and allows cold to infiltrate the heated indoors; in the summer, when you want to be able to open and close your windows to get fresh air, the wood expands and the windows swell shut.

Aluminum and steel have strength. You can manufacture windows made of these materials to fit any opening. These windows, however, have a major drawback, which is called through-to-through conductivity. That is, the transfer of cold air meeting warm air masses forms condensation. The bottom line is these windows conduct heat and cold.

Vinyl has a great insulation value, and it is virtually maintenance free. However, in some cases, vinyl is not final. Vinyl comes in different grades, and it must be reinforced to be effective. Vinyl has a degradation factor, and if it goes out of shape, it doesn't return to its original state.

These examples simply show advantage and disadvantage among products. We are not knocking other products; we are only giving the factual pros and cons of different products. This is the correct way to eliminate competition.

Let's continue using windows as an example. You can later apply the same principle and use the same simple breakdown to your product.

Glass makes up about 89 percent of a window. There are several types of glass on the market today. These types of glass fall into one of two categories. The first category is foreign or rolled glass, which is unstable because it contains high marks, low marks, and imperfections. If I sandwiched three panes of foreign or rolled glass together, looking through them would be like looking through a Coke bottle. So I can't use foreign glass when I'm multi-layering glass.

The second category of glass is float glass, the best glass on the market. Float glass costs a few dollars more, but it is worth it? *Yes*; it's the finest glass on the market today.

There are all kinds of multi-layering products. Alternatives include single pane, 1/2-inch double pane, 1-inch double pane, triple pane, triple pane with argon gas, triple pane with krypton gas, or heat mirror.

Once again, we want to show the characteristics of every type of glass using a heat lamp demonstration, which shows the amount of heat that comes through each glass type. The more panes of layered glass, the less heat will transfer through, which in turn means a better product. The better the product, the more you save on energy costs. This means the product is more expensive on the initial investment but a better buy in the long run. *Yes*, it cost a few dollars more initially, but isn't it worth that extra cost?

As in this example, many products can be expensive to own initially and turn out to be a real investment in the long run. We have all heard the phrase "your initial investment cost." This is the path you want to take with the product you sell. You want be able to say, "Mr. and Mrs. Prospect, most of the products you buy today end up costing you money over time. But the product I'm showing you is an investment, not an expenditure."

Price Justification Creates Higher Retail Value

Here is the long and short of it: If you want to sell your product to the exclusion of all other products out there, you must create a perceived value to your prospects that is higher than the product's retail value. You have to make the product worth more to prospects than what you are selling it for, or you will never sell it.

How do we sell a window for $700? We make it worth $1,400. And it is worth every penny of that because it is one of the very few products available that includes a 40 percent fuel-savings pledge, or our company will pay the difference.

Whenever I present this product to prospects, I say:

> Mr. and Mrs. Prospect, if you don't put these windows in, let me tell you what will happen. I will come back here seven years from today, knock on your door, and say, "Today is the day you could have owned windows instead of receipts from the gas and electric company!"

This kind of jargon is important for prospects to hear, so they can realize exactly what they are letting themselves in for. One other thing I try to impress upon prospects is this:

> Mr. and Mrs. Prospect, please understand that you are never going to go to the mailbox and look at your utility bill and say, "Thank God, I just paid the last one!" However, if you finance these windows, 36 months from now you will make your last payment and continue to save 40 percent on your gas or electric bill.

Be Aware of Current Events

You must also be aware of current events that might stimulate sales of your product; for example, in our business, the high cost of heating oil and natural gas. Pending war with Iraq also has fuel costs fluctuating and ready to soar.

If your product has a pay-back period, it certainly would be to your advantage to hock it. Knowing that prospects are investing in your product rather than buying your product is definitely a perceived advantage to them.

Romance Your Product

When prospects ask me, "How much does your product cost?" I reply, "What if I told you I could give it to you for free? What would you say?" I wait for a reaction, and then I proceed to tell them:

> This product is one of the few that can save you enough money to compensate for your expenditure in just a few years. And in future years, it will continue to yield you a return. Understand that the initial investment is a few dollars more, but isn't it worth it?

In every selling situation, prospects will turn to alternatives if they are not convinced that your product can and will do what you say it does. Confidence selling plays an important role in the competitive market place. The salesperson who is thoroughly convincing will win prospects over, earn their trust, and gain their business.

Trust is the key word in this statement. To repeat what I said earlier, people need to trust you to do business with you. To trust you, they must be convinced, and you can accomplish this only by eliminating all competition.

You eliminate competition by demonstrating what prospects need to be cognizant of when it comes time for them to purchase a product. Make sure that you touch on each and every product feature. Doing this is called *romancing the product*. People need to fall in love with your product, and that process depends on you.

Break Down Costs to Kill Options

We've talked a great deal already about price conditioning. One thing I like to do when my product is up against an inexpensive product is to break down into all the components how much it costs to make the inexpensive product. I start with:

> Mr. and Mrs. Prospect, let's look at the flow of the product. Let's say the retailer needs to get $300 for it. The retailer buys the product from the wholesaler for about half of that, let's say $150. But the retailer has

to put its markup on the product—it wants to maintain a profit of 50 percent.

The wholesaler has bought the product from the distributor for about 50 percent of the wholesale price, or $75. The wholesaler also had to put its markup on the product, which is about double what the wholesaler paid for it.

The distributor bought the product from the manufacturer for $36.50, because the distributor also has to make money, and so it has put its 100 percent markup on it.

The original material and labor cost to manufacture the product is about 80 percent, or $29.20, of the manufacturer's selling price of $36.50. This means the manufacture is working for less than 20 percent actual profit, or less than $6.80, for this product. You can't even buy lunch for that amount of money.

How could anyone manufacture a quality piece of goods at that price?

People can relate to this breakdown if you use a piece of paper to illustrate the retailer, the wholesaler, the distributor, and the manufacturer.

As a salesperson, the best situation to be in is when your product comes directly from the manufacturer to you, with no middlemen and no hidden costs. This is the position we are in at Homeview Contractors Inc., and it's much easier to sell the concept and our product from this vantage point. You want to be able to say, "We make it, we ship it, we service it, we install it, we guarantee it—all under one roof, from raw material to finished product, designed exclusively for you." With this setup, all the money goes directly into the product rather than into other people's pockets as they put their markup on it.

To kill options for prospects, the qualifying questions are the most significant questions you will ever ask. You use these qualifiers to cater to the prospects' wants and desires. Your qualifying questions consist of the various key elements we've discussed in this chapter. From what you've read, you can now develop a list of qualifying questions to ask.

And remember that eliciting all this information from prospects will also be of great help when you're ready to close the sale. The prospects responses throughout this process will show you exactly how they wish to be sold. I think of it as playing poker and being allowed to peek into everyone's hands to see whether you want to bet or fold.

Use Word Target Responses

Again, using qualifiers to get prospects accustomed to saying *Yes* is vitally important. You need to gear all qualifying questions so they will produce either a *Yes* response or a *word target response*. One word target response you might try to invoke, for example, is *energy savings*. Let's try it. "Mr. and Mrs. Prospect, when it comes time to purchase a product, will you be looking for beauty or for something that will give you tremendous *energy savings* and thus save you thousands of dollars?" Hopefully, they will say, "Both." If they do, you will come back to them with "If you had to pick one, which would it be?"

Early on in the presentation you use many different techniques; for instance, price conditioning. As you should know by now, price conditioning should start at Step 1, as soon as you walk to the door, and continue to the close. Combine target word response with price conditioning for the greatest impact.

Positive Mental Attitude (PMA)

When sales representatives fall into a slump, they immediately feel as if they've lost their sales talent. To turn the situation around, all they need to do is go back to the basics—you know, the 10-step sales

SALES PRO TIP

You Never Lose Your Ability; You Just Lose Your Attitude
Selling is all about attitude. Without the proper attitude, you will find selling a tough row to hoe.

presentation, and all the things that worked so well they stopped using them. Selling is repetition. For example, you are seeing many repetitive statements throughout this book. That's because the material must hit home, and you must able to use this information consistently. If you can do that, it will be only a matter of time before the closing becomes natural and much easier for you. You see, when you work the sales plan, good things happen to you.

Remember that you never lose your sales ability; you just lose your attitude. Selling is all about attitude. Without the proper attitude, you will find selling a tough row to hoe.

How do you prepare to have the proper attitude in a sale presentation? Is there some sort of magic formula to bring about success in selling? *Positive Mental Attitude*, or *PMA*, is the single possession that will help you accomplish whatever it is you want to accomplish in life.

Whenever I feel down, or not up to par, I repeat the following saying three times. Doing so makes me feel great. These words have changed my mood and my life on many of occasions:

> Henceforth, I grow more good-humored. Joy, happiness, and cheerfulness are now becoming my normal, natural state of mind. Every day I'm becoming more and more loveable and understanding. I am now becoming the center of cheer and goodwill to all those around me, infecting them with good humor. This happy, joyous, cheerful mood is now becoming my normal, natural state of mind. I am grateful.

Repeat this saying three times, and your mood will also change from bad to good. I guarantee—it works.

To make the sales game work, you must have a great attitude. If you follow the steps outline in this book, you stand a good chance of making a six-figure income, or at least very close to it.

SALES PRO TIP

Positive Mental Attitude (PMA) is Essential
With PMA, you can accomplish whatever you want to accomplish.

Product Demonstration

- Show and Tell

- Create Believability

- Use Humor

- Involvement

- Price Condition

- Use FAB

- Build Value

- Show Functionality with Beauty

- Solicit Feedback from Prospect

- Use Qualifying Questions

STEP 6

Product Presentation

The Ten Step Selling Plan

STEP 1
Entry

STEP 2
Warm-up

STEP 3
Create Need

STEP 4
Company Story

STEP 5
Kill Options

STEP 6
Product Presentation
Show and Tell
Price Condition
Qualifying Questions

STEP 7
Pre-Close

STEP 8
Close

STEP 9
Post Close

STEP 10
Replace the Lead

The single most important part of your entire sales presentation is the product demonstration. The concept that you must sell your product to all other products out there originates here. The demonstration is the time when prospects decide whether they have a genuine need for your product or will pass on your offer. Establishing a pre-price conception and justifying the price to your prospects, and comparing the parts and pieces of your product to the competitions' parts and pieces are all of the utmost importance now.

At this point, you have hopefully killed all other options and will present your product in an orderly way, so that prospects will understand why it is much better and more efficient than the others.

Talk, Prove, and Show

More and more places of business are offering people hands-on experi-

SALES PRO TIP

To Get the Dough, You Must Do the Show
People respect a sales representative who covers all the bases. They enjoy watching someone do a great product demonstration.

ence in using their products. Retail stores have the products they sell on display, ready for use. They are not willing to simply show the product or talk about it; they want to be able to demonstrate it. And for that brief moment, as the potential prospects try out the products, they assume ownership.

As you demonstrate your product to prospects, showing how good the product is isn't enough; you must show how good your product is *for these prospects*. You must talk, prove, and show, and the only good way to do that is by doing a great product demonstration.

Every demonstration is divided into two stages. The first stage revolves around the first part of the sales presentation, and the second stage involves the actual physical demonstration of the product. These two stages go hand and hand. They both must be interesting. More importantly, they both must be convincing to the prospects for them to make a buying decision.

You must convey to the prospects the product's convenience and beauty, and how much time, work, energy, money, or whatever else your product will save them.

The 10 Commandments of Selling

Now is a good time to introduce you to the 10 Commandments of Selling, some of which will already be familiar to you:

1. Nothing the prospects will say or do will discourage you from making a complete and thorough presentation.
2. Always be respectful of the prospects.

3. Never short-cut the presentation.
4. Always listen to the prospects.
5. Keep the prospects involved in your presentation.
6. Always use third-party influence.
7. Never high-pressure prospects.
8. Never sell something that shouldn't be sold.
9. Sell your product to the exclusion of all others!
10. Never prejudge prospects, affordability, or a selling situation.

Samples Sell

The product demonstration consists of "See me, feel me, and understand me." You must make sure you are explicit when you demonstrate your product. For the product demonstration, you must carry with you at all times a group of sample cases with your product broken down inside them. No matter what you're selling, the product sample must be in a disassembled state. Each and every screw, spring, rivet, partial piece of material, fabric sample, and cut section of the actual product must be ready for presentation.

And as long as they won't harm prospects, you should have at your disposal, and demonstrate, any type of common household chemicals that might damage other products. You want to show that the other products will rust, oxidize, wear, or will do anything else that would make prospects think twice about purchasing them. For example, have pieces of your competitions' products that have been subjected to inclement weather conditions.

Keep the Flow

The series of events in your presentation should follow a standardized pattern and logical sequence for prospects to understand, and you need to do the presentation exactly the same way time after time. Throughout the demonstration, prospects must be able to say, "I can see how that feature in your product is so much better than anything else I have seen, and better than anything else you have shown me in other companies' samples."

Throughout your presentation, narrow down the selections and zero in on your product. You want your product to stand alone. And a product doesn't just get to be a standalone product—you have to present it in such a way that it becomes one.

Some people think they can shortcut the product demonstration. But to do so is a serious mistake that is likely to lead to a failure to convert the demonstration into a sale. Salespeople often think they are boring the prospects when they start their presentation. Just remember: you might have seen or done the product demonstration a thousand times. But this is probably the first time the prospects have seen a complete product demo.

Comfort Zone

The first hurdle you are up against in your demonstration is that people generally resist change. Prospects are reluctant to come out of their comfort zones, so you must give them reasons to convince them that they should. To help you do this, you should be aware of the major reasons prospects resist change:

- Fear of making a decision about money or of committing to such a decision.
- Fear of the unknown.
- Fear of admitting to you that they have no money on hand.
- Fear that this is a scam and they will lose their money.
- Fear of realizing they were pressured by you into buying something. (Your goal is for them to feel the pressure was from within and that the decision was truly their decision.)
- Fear of losing face.
- Fear of losing their job in the future.
- Fear of financial rejection.
- Fear of committing to a monthly payment.
- Fear of change.

Your goal is to convince your prospects, through your demonstration and by following through on your sales plan, that their fears are unfounded.

Trust is a Must

I talked earlier about how important it is to earn prospects' trust by being truthful about your product and your company. You also must establish trust to fend off prospects' fears. Trust is the basis for 85 percent of all major buying decisions, even though prospects use product price as their major point of resistance and the deterrent to investing. Prospects always talk "lowest and cheapest price," but what they really want is quality and good service.

Remember that people will never take any significant action unless you have stimulated an emotion in them. The two emotions that are most important in this regard are passion and fear. Triggering these two emotions is vital, because they both create anxiety. And the quickest way for us to stimulate prospects is to create anxiety. For example, fear of loss helps them move more quickly into admitting that they have a potential problem, and they will react faster to find a solution to solve that problem. If you are in the roofing business and can honestly convince prospects that unless they soon replace their roof, for instance, they are likely to incur major expenses in terms of structural damage, interior ceiling and wall damage, and the like, you are well on you way to a close.

Many sales representatives have great presentation skills but weak closing skills. They can stir emotions, but they fail to close. And later, when they follow up, they find that the prospects have bought from elsewhere. Once you have stimulated prospects' anxiety, your job as a professional sales representative is to relieve them of this anxiety with your knowledge of your company and your product. You must build prospects' trust and value in you, your company, and your product, alleviate their fear of commitment, and lead them to a positive decision.

Contagious Enthusiasm

Once again, your goal is to get prospects out of their comfort zones, stimulate their emotions, awaken their anxieties, and let them admit they need to take affirmative action so they can return to their comfort zones.

When you demonstrate your product, use vocabulary such as "What you are about to see is truly amazing!" Enthusiasm is contagious. Be enthused about your product, and prospects will sense your excitement. If people really understood the power of enthusiasm, they would use it all the time.

Some people say, "To be enthusiastic you must act enthusiastic." I feel differently about enthusiasm, however, and I believe there is a right way and a wrong way to use it. Enthusiasm must be natural, because your prospects know when it's not genuine.

Sincerity also is vital to maintain a captivated audience. But unlike enthusiasm, sincerity is a character or personality trait rather than an emotional state. While it is true that a sales representative might sell a product without a sincere interest in the prospects, a key factor in consistently selling yourself or your product is that buyers recognize you are genuinely sincere. Unlike enthusiasm, you can't "put on" sincerity. You either are sincere or you aren't. If you are just acting sincere, most prospects will read through your phony act.

Also understand that even though you can't "put on" sincerity, it can develop. If you honestly believe in your product or service as the best on the market, then you can honestly believe you are providing a genuine service to prospects. If you have this perspective, you are beginning to develop sincerity.

Drive It Around the Block

When you demonstrate your product, make sure you include a series of tests that you can show to your prospects. These could include tests to show strength, durability, or how well the product performs in heat or cold.

No matter what you are selling; you can always find numerous ways to show how well your product is made. Think of the demo as a show-and-tell session. The key is always to be prepared. The more ammunition you have, the more likely you are to hit your target.

You should outline the series of steps to the demonstration in a presentation book of some sort that closely follows the flow of the demonstration. Sometimes, I have seen sales representatives hand prospects a sheet of paper that outlines the points of the product demonstration. This format keeps everyone singing from the same song sheet, and no one misses a beat. For example, you can hand the paper to the prospects and say:

> Mr. and Mrs. Prospect, I want to make sure I don't miss anything when I present our product to you. I want you to learn as much as possible so that when it comes time to make a decision, you will be well informed. If you would, please do me a favor and call off the first feature on the list, and I will point that out to you. And then I will explain the feature to you so you understand how it will benefit you. Fair enough? What's that first feature on the list?

This is one way to go about a factual and well-orchestrated product demonstration.

Another way is to carry a parts kit into the prospects' home and pull out each and every part that comprises your product. Include a thorough explanation of each component's material and how that will be of benefit to the prospects.

Parts kits are of the utmost importance so prospects can touch the pieces, feel strength, and look at the finish. Use each of the five senses to get your point across in a product demonstration. Talking, showing, smelling, tasting, touching, listening, painting word pictures—all these stimulate the brain and the imagination.

You might wonder how you would use sound in selling your product. Let's use windows again as our product in a sample statement:

> Mr. and Mrs. Prospect, you see how easy it is to tilt this window in for easy cleaning? Now I want you to listen when I close it. Notice that I don't have to be gentle. [I proceed to slam the window.] Hear that? It sounds like a Cadillac door closing, doesn't it?

Practice Makes Perfect

You must constantly role-play the product demonstration. Practice does make perfect, and perfect makes for easy closing. You should constantly add new pieces to freshen up your approach and remove old methods from your presentation that did not produce the expected results.

Striving for perfection is a never-ending battle. One cannot do things the same way each and every day and expect enhanced results. You must constantly change the way you do things. Every day, try to learn something new from somebody or something. Then try to incorporate this new experience into your daily ritual. Some people truly believe that only time changes; they have no concept of changing times. But you must keep up with changing times to be competitive in the marketplace.

Keep Pace

Everyone has something to sell that he or she feels is bigger, better, and less costly than yours. That is why competition is good in today's marketplace. Your competitors share in the promotional costs of your product through their advertising, and as they try to sell their products, they enlighten consumers to the need of having a product just like yours. Your competitors are out daily, spreading the word about how well their products work, products they feel are identical to and even better than the one you're selling.

SALES PRO TIP

Keep Pace to Win the Race
To compete and win in the sales game, you must keep pace. You must have the right tools at the right time and communicate professionally to prospects at all times.

Always remember that everything has a price tag, regardless of what it is or who owns it. As long as the price is right or the expenditure is justifiable, goods will continue to be bought and sold each and every day.

What I described is simply the sales game in action. If you want to be a part of it, you must learn to keep pace. Keeping pace means having the right tools at the right time, and communicating at all times in a professional, business-like manner to prospects.

Keep this principle in mind as you lead your prospects down the road to the close. Always be professional. Sales representatives often feel they should act as though they know everything. Nobody likes the "know-it-all," but everybody appreciates and respects those who know what they should know. And while any knowledge you might have about a subject may help you relate to prospects, the most important knowledge you can demonstrate is your knowledge about your product.

To develop this professional atmosphere about you, you must learn everything about your product and how it will benefit the prospects. This knowledge, coupled with self-confidence, will yield you great rewards in terms of financial stability and riches beyond belief.

The Kill Book

Internet access has made building a kill book easy. Now, instead of visiting every one of your competitors, you never have to leave your computer. The Internet information pool is endless and readily available, and you can turn your computer into a money-making machine by doing the necessary research your selling job requires. The information you can print out is unbelievable.

Just about any company worth its salt has an Internet site. Making use of all this available information is the proper way to build a great selling portfolio. Good sales representatives know who and what they are up against when it comes to product. What better way for you to become educated than visiting other companies' websites to research their products? You can research every component, alloy, or space age material in competitors' products as well as your own. You become the authority, and people will gain more respect for you and your company as a result of the wealth of knowledge you possess.

The Best of the Rest

When you present your product to prospects, it is all right to assume that they have seen other products. You do this by saying, "Mr. and Mrs. Prospect, I'm sure this isn't the first time someone has shown you what they felt was a great product. However, you have seen the rest, and I'm about to show you the best. Fair enough?"

This assumption will lead prospects to admit either that they have seen other products or that this is the first time. Through this process, if prospects have seen other products, you will be able to find out how much they think those products are worth.

Sell the Difference

Selling a difference between what prospects feel products are worth is much easier than selling the entire dollar value of your product. Here's an example: you are able to extract from prospects that the price quoted to them for a competitor's product was $5,000. The price for your product is $7,000. It is much easier for you to justify

SALES PRO TIP

Trade Up by Trading Down
Remember to start at the top of the line for your product, explaining features, advantages, and benefits, and then drop down to lower-priced versions from there. Also, you can more easily justify price if you assign a dollar value to each product feature—price condition early and often.

the $2,000 difference between the two products than it is to sell prospects on a $7,000 starting price for your product.

That's also why price conditioning, which we've discussed several times already, is so important. Go through the product breakdown and assign a price to each piece. Then, when prospects tell you they were quoted a price that was $2,000 less, you can say, "Mr. and Mrs. Prospect, remember when I asked whether you would rather have a material that won't weather well, like the other product you saw, and you told me that a better material was important to you?"

Their answer should be a strong "Yes." This is an example of the importance of mini-commitments, and of getting prospects to say *Yes* as often as you can.

Notice what happens in the conversation now:

> To have this option of improved, weather-resistant material available to you, you would have to invest approximately $750 more, which would mean a total investment of about $75 a year for a 10-year period of time. Would it be worth that to you?

Notice what I just did. I broke the price difference down to the miniscule, or the ridiculous. I want the flurries of *Yes* responses to continue. Now I say:

> Mr. and Mrs. Prospect, remember that I said price buyers are twice buyers. We build our product so this will be the first and last time you will have to make this purchase. For us to do this, you will have to invest about $450 more up front, but in a 10-year period, your total investment is only $45 more per year. Is the better product worth that to you?

Again, I am looking for that *Yes* answer. And if you notice, I have already justified $1,200 of the $2,000 price difference between the competitor's product and mine. All I need to do is use my product's other features, advantages, and benefits to come up with the remaining $800.

All I have done is to go through the process of price justification, which works especially well when the competition has already given the prospects a demonstration. But I'm sure you also want to know how to handle prospects who have never been given another demonstration or price.

Again, you must price condition as you talk about your product:

> "Mr. and Mrs. Prospect, when you purchase this product, remember that service will be very important to you. A small $15 or $20 part could go bad, and if the company doesn't provide excellent customer service, the product you just spent $7,000 for is worthless!"

Another approach is just to mention the price other companies are charging for their similar products. You can get price comparisons from the Internet, and then you might start by saying:

> Mr. and Mrs. Prospect, the product I'm about to show you will make your life so much easier. Here are some of the products that try to emulate ours. Consider Companies X, Y, and Z, and you can see that Company X is charging $4,000 for its product. Company Y comes in with a price of $5,499, and Company Z is selling its product for $3,800. My only suggestion to you is that if you don't buy from us, buy from somebody like us. All the companies I have mentioned are great companies; however, let me show you the difference between what you will get from us and what you can expect from them!

Absorb Shock

Notice that I have set out three separate prices for them to absorb. When I quote my price later, after I have thoroughly justified my product, the fact that they already have these other prices in mind will lessen the blow, or the sticker shock, of my product's price. If I don't do this, the prospects will tend to respond to my price information with "Just leave your card, and we will get back with you."

If you get such a response, you might be tempted to say something like "Mr. and Mrs. Prospect, I don't have a card with me, but here's what I will do. When I get back to the office, I will take one of my cards and rip it up and throw it in the garbage for you. That will save you the trouble of doing it yourself. How does that sound to you?" But I wouldn't recommend it. I use this example to prove the point that you will never get back in their home once prospects blow you off.

Failure Leads to Excuses

One thing I teach is that making excuses can be a direct result of failure. When you don't close a sale, don't use excuses such as the people were jerks and wouldn't buy anything from anyone. Or that the people weren't interested right now; we have to call them back next year. Or they told you they don't have the money to do anything. No selling organization should tolerate excuses. Always remember: "Excuses satisfy only those who make them!"—no one else.

Why Buy

When you present your product, you need to understand that prospects will buy for many different reasons. Prospects are motivated to buy your product only for one or more of these six reasons:

1. **Desire for Gain** (making money on their investment)
2. **Fear** of **Loss** (whether the loss is personal, family, home, or money)
3. **Security** and **Protection** (personal, family, or home)
4. **Comfort** and **Convenience** (personal, family, or home)
5. **Pride** of **Ownership** (personal)
6. **Emotional Satisfaction** (to maintain dignity; personal)

Your goal must be to zero in on prospects' hot buttons. People will make a decision if you can appeal to one or more of the above.

Keep It Under Control

Always remember that people hate to buy but love to own. A majority of the time, we believe that prospects are concerned about the price of our product. But price does not sell a job or product—a great sales representative does. The only person who is really concerned about price is the sales representative. That's why you must justify the price to yourself and to your prospects.

As salespersons, we too might have a tendency to shy away from quoting a price because we feel we are charging too much and prospects are going to say *No* to our offer. But don't lowball a price because you feel prospects will think that the higher price is too much money. If you're going to think negatively, do yourself a favor and stop thinking, because it will only get you in trouble.

Think about this again: "The body manifests what the mind harbors." If you think you can, or you think you can't, you're right. The result or outcome of this statement will be in direct proportion to what you think. When you have control of the selling situation, your thought processes are far different than if you lose control. Your confidence level reaches an all-time high when you have complete control from start to finish.

And as long as you follow the sales plan, keeping control is fairly easy. I firmly believe this, and it's the job of this book to get you to not only believe it but also put it into practice as quickly as you can. The sooner you do, the sooner you will increase your sales and establish more control in the selling situation than you have ever had before.

Good Habits

Most people I have taught to work this sales plan make in excess of $80,000 to $100,000 a year. Some have gone on to own their own businesses and be extremely successful. All I did was give them the sales plan and how to use it; they committed the steps to memory, implemented the process, and used the plan daily.

When you do something religiously every day, you can develop new habits—good habits. But you must do them consistently, day after day.

As an example, it generally takes a person six times to commit something such as a first and last name to memory. I have been told this from real estate agents who used the following example: If you knock on people's doors and introduce yourself, first and last name, they will not remember your name when you leave. If you go back the next day and introduce yourself again using first and last name, they still will not remember your name. When you go back the third day, they will probably remember the first letter of your first name. The fourth day when you go back, they will know your first name and will pause as if they almost remember your last name, but they probably don't. The fifth time you go back, they will know your first name and the first letter of your last name. The sixth time you go back, they will have committed your first and last name to memory.

Knowing this, think of all the things you say once in the sales presentation and expect prospects to remember. Again, how many times do you brush over how your product works and expect prospects to remember? Prospects will not remember statements you make only once, so don't expect them to. The sales presentation is geared for prospects to hear statements about how your product works more than one time. The sales plan is redundant on purpose, so prospect can absorb the good parts of the presentation.

The product demonstration is the highlight of your sales visit. By this step, you should have done the necessary things to "Create Need," sold your prospects on the professionalism of "Your Company," and done a great job of "Killing Options" and proving the value of your product.

Without this kind of up-front setup, the close will be virtually impossible. You must do the front end to get to the back end and get the sell. And you must do the same thing time and time again so you can become so proficient at it that it becomes second nature. Then and only then will you have mastered the art of closing a sale.

Pre-Close

- ● **Create Urgency**

- ● **Establish Payment Plans**

- ● **Schedule Time Frame**

- ● **Explain—in Detail—What the Prospect Will Be Provided**

- ● **Build Value**

- ● **Assume the Sale**

- ● **Ask: Is There a Reason Other Than Price That Would Keep Us from Completing an Order Today?**

- ● **Retail Price Quote**

STEP 7

Pre-Close

STEP 1
Entry

STEP 2
Warm-up

STEP 3
Create Need

STEP 4
Company Story

STEP 5
Kill Options

STEP 6
Product Presentation

STEP 7
Pre-Close
Retail Price Quote
Work Out Budget
Set Up Urgency

STEP 8
Close

STEP 9
Post Close

STEP 10
Replace the Lead

The pre-close involves overcoming objections and conditions, working out the retail price quote and a budget for prospects, and creating urgency as a basis for them to do business with your company today.

To Be Back Is to Be Broke

I made this statement earlier in reference to closing: "To be back is to be broke." This means that you always want to first-call close prospects. You do this by setting up urgency for prospects to take advantage of what you have to offer on the first visit. And you offer additional incentives to make this happen.

During the course of the presentation, you bring your prospects to a new level of excitement. What better time for them to take advantage of something than when it's fresh in their mind? The prospects are well educated on the company and the

SALES PRO TIP

Focus on First-Call Close
First-call close means you walk into a house as a total stranger and walk out two or three hours later with a contract and a check. Good first-call closers believe "To be back is to be broke."

product, thanks to you, and they can now make an informative decision about investing in your product. You've set the mood, the prospects are eagerly awaiting the price, and you are eagerly waiting to give that price so you can go to close.

It's now or never for you to attain the necessary results to move to the first-call close. You need the prospect to have substantial belief in your company, in your product, and—most importantly—in you. You need the prospects' trust when you move to close this deal.

Remember that in the warm-up, only open-ended questions are allowed. As you move through the sales plan toward the close, however, you can and want to use close-ended questions. Some of these questions might be "Can you see, Mr. and Mrs. Prospect, how this product can literally save you thousands of dollars?" or "Can you see, Mr. and Mrs. Prospect, how this product can be of daily benefit to you?" You want questions such as these to trigger a *Yes* response.

SALES PRO TIP

Ask Close-Ended Questions Toward the Close
Ask close-ended questions as you move toward the close, to keep prospects repeating the word yes. When prospects get used to saying **Yes**, **Yes** will be much easier for them to say as you move to the close.

Get Back to Yes

You have managed to question prospects using phrases to elicit that *Yes* response. You have used phrases such as "Didn't you?", "Isn't it?", "Wouldn't you?", "Don't you agree?", "Isn't that correct?", "Shouldn't it?", "Can't you?", "Wasn't it?", "Doesn't it?", "Aren't they?", "Couldn't it?", and ". . . a few dollars more, but isn't it worth it?" All these are Yes-producing statements.

In an earlier chapter we talked about the principle of reinforcement and feedback. Here is your golden opportunity to put this principle into practice. You must always listen to what the prospects want or like, and then make a mental note to reinforce that information and provide relevant feedback to them later in the sales process.

Let's say the prospects state, "Security has become a major concern in this neighborhood." Now you will go for the *Yes* response, and reinforce and provide feedback at the same time. "You did say security is a major issue in this neighborhood, didn't you?"

The prospects answer, "Yes."

You then proceed with "Great! I'm so glad you appreciate the security elements we have manufactured and designed into our product to give you complete peace of mind!"

Make It Natural

This sales process will eventually become natural for you to use. But it will become natural only if you study and apply it. When you do so, you will gain positive sales performance.

When the sales plan is unnatural to use, you will not obtain definitive results. I cannot stress this enough. If you don't understand the sales plan, or you don't make an effort and habitually practice this systematic approach to selling, then hang it up, my friend. The sales game is not the right profession for you.

Persistence Breaks Resistance

Remember that you must never settle for the first **No** prospects say to you. You must be ready to answer their stall in a way that won't offend but that will keep the flow of the conversation going, to bring them closer to a **Yes**.

You have the right to tell your prospects all the things they would be missing out on if they didn't invest in your product. I'm not saying to go into their home and whine and nag. I am saying to make sure that when prospects say No, they mean No. Just as a steady flow of water will erode a large boulder, a bit of persistence will overcome stalls.

Accepting Resistance

Throughout your entire sales presentations, you must accept resistance and being put off—from the time you battled your way into the prospects' home, through that initial wall of resistance at the door, to the resistance you faced in the warm-up, as you created need and eliminated alternatives, and during the product demonstration.

Get used to fighting an uphill battle. Just remember: once you reach the top of the hill, the rest of the way will be downhill. Be patient, and learn to accept the sales process as a regimented way of life—nothing more, nothing less.

I have never been in a selling situation in which I didn't hear many No responses before I heard a *Yes*. I can assure you that you will receive resistance and be put off, before, during, and after the sales presentation. The difference is that successful sales representatives accept this as part of the law of selling. Prospects do not mean to balk on a proposal, or to create excuses and stalls. You must learn to understand that they do this because they have fears, apprehensions, and uncertainties.

Prospects are faced with the fear of making the wrong decision. The problem lies with the sales representative who reads this fear as prospects not wanting the product—or, even worse, that prospects are not even interested in the product. Another common misperception on the part of the salesperson is that the prospect does not need the product, or that the sales representative just wasted his or her time on a worthless appointment set up by an incompetent person (more commonly referred to as a "bad lead").

Dodging Arrows

Train yourself to think of prospect resistance this way: prospects have a quill of arrows, and they will use these arrows to wound you throughout the entire sales presentation. When they tell you up front that they are not interested in your product and you are wasting your time, they have removed an arrow from their quill, put it on the string of the bow, pulled back the string, and released the arrow, which results in a direct hit to your heart. If you let them, wounds from these stray arrows can deplete the blood supply and take the life out of your sales presentation—and ultimately do the same to you. Objections, put offs, and general sales resistance are all part of the arrows that wound the already vulnerable, weak salesperson. (This is the sales representative who is constantly looking for another job with a new company where things will be "better.")

You must not let these arrows affect you, however. Remember that "Nothing a customer will say or do will discourage me. . ."—not only from making a complete and thorough product demonstration, but also from successfully completing your sales plan. Proceed with your presentation, and let prospects fire their arrows at will. At some point, they will reach into their quill and find no arrows left to fire. You can then proceed to the close without further complications or fear of being hit by any more arrows.

SALES PRO TIP

Always Remember
The things dreams are made from don't become reality until action is applied.

Drawing the Line

A fine line exists between success and failure in the sales presentation. You choose the route you wish to take, and your choice will prove either financially rewarding or financially devastating. When you go into prospects' homes, be there to win. If you win, everyone wins. Prospects win because they have the finest product money can buy. They also have a company that stands behind them in service. You win because you accomplished what you set out to accomplish, and your company wins because it has made a profit on what you have sold. The manufacturer wins because the company has to place the order there, and the manufacturer has to make a profit. Your family wins because it reaps the rewards of the commission dollars you make by selling the product. Your creditors win because you can now make the monthly mortgage payment. It's a win-win situation for everyone involved.

Objections and Conditions

Next, you need to understand *objections* and *conditions*. Objections and conditions are both merely stalls that prospects use in the sales presentation to sidestep the decision-making process. These objections and conditions can be fatal to weak, uncommitted, or untrained sales representatives.

Let's define an objection. An objection is a real, valid reason in prospects' minds for not continuing with the sales presentation.

The first time you hear an objection, it is generally wise to let it pass. You might choose to let the objection pass because you have been price conditioning the prospects several times. They have already determined in their own minds that they cannot afford your product, based on that price conditioning. But you might not have gone over the entire presentation yet; and later, when you justify why you charge what you charge, the prospects will understand, and their fears and apprehensions will be alleviated.

Prospects' objections become a reflex action, like the jerk of their knees when a doctor hits them with a mallet. The prospects don't know how to shut your sales presentation down otherwise, so they will use knee-jerk reactions and throw some objections out there to slow the selling process. These objections seemed to work extremely well when they used them on the weaker sales representative before you, so why shouldn't they use them again?

Conditions Stall Decisions

Conditions are stalls that might be real; conditions always involve third-party influence. Prospects state conditions to discourage you. Conditions let them continue to not make a decision.

There are only five reasons why prospects will set up a condition, and they all relate to something that went awry in your sales presentation. If prospects present conditions, you did not succeed in one or more of the following areas:

- Reducing fear
- Creating urgency
- Building value in your product or company
- Creating affordability
- Establishing trust

Unfortunately, it's important to realize that you will not sell everyone. At the same time, your mission and goal should always be to qualify prospects, create excitement during the product demonstration, and close the sale in the process.

If you do this continuously, your close rate should be at least 33 percent, or one close out of every three presentations. If you receive three to four additional *No* responses, you should increase your close rate by another 17 percent, improving it to 50 percent.

Price and Terms

Understand that all prospect objections narrow down to only two things—price and terms. If I had a funnel that separated the following objections into groups, and I put all the objections into the funnel, they would land either in the price pile or the terms pile:

"I might be selling the house."

"I need to buy a new car."

"I want to think about this; I will get back to you."

"I want to get several more estimates."

"I need to talk this over with my son or daughter."

"I don't do anything until I sleep on it."

"I don't know what I have to pay in federal tax; I need to get back to you."

"The roof on my house is leaking; I have to have that replaced first."

"I'm too old to make that kind of investment."

"I really want to wait till the stock market does better."

"I might be laid off next week; I'll have to wait and see."

"I don't know what my health is like; I have a doctor's appointment later this month."

"I want to wait till I have the money to pay cash."

I could go on forever, but the objections all narrow down to price and terms. Put as many excuses, stalls, or whatever you want to call them into the wide mouth of the funnel, and rest assured that price and terms will be all that filters through.

Running the Budget

If prospects feel that the investment is right, and they can afford your product without dipping into the proverbial cookie jar, then you have a deal. And how can you tell if they really can afford it? Ask them. You're not a mind reader, and educated guesses don't work in this business. You must run a budget for prospects.

Here's how it works. "Mr. and Mrs. Prospect, what is your mortgage payment? I pay about $1,800 a month." Prospects will usually tell you exactly what they pay in dollars and cents because you told them what you pay. If you say, "I know you have a car payment. My car costs me about $575 a month. What do you pay?" again, they will tell you. Why? Because you divulged how much you pay.

Do this on all items such as insurance, food, utilities, gas, luxury purchases, and other incidentals such as health clubs and the like. Ask prospects approximately how much they bring in per month, and compare that amount to what they spend. Add the price of your product as a monthly installment, and then present the results to them.

> Mr. and Mrs. Prospect, you have approximately $4,300 combined coming in monthly, and $2,800 going out. That leaves you with $1,500 of disposable income that can go into your savings account. The numbers I just ran include the monthly installment on my product."

When you can show people they can afford your product, they are more likely to listen and invest if the price and terms are agreeable.

Presenting the Price—with Urgency

When I talk about quoting the price, I don't mean simply throwing a price on the table and waiting for prospects to say *Yes*. You must take a series of steps before you quote the price. When I talked about the funnel, I was talking about comments coming from the prospects' mouths being filtered through the funnel. You are going to challenge the prospects, to see whether you can elicit some of these objections earlier, so they don't come up later in the presentation and kill the deal.

A question you want to ask is "Would there be any other reason, other than price, why we can't get together on an order for my product today?" You do this before you do the price presentation. *Yes*, even the price has a geared presentation. The first thing you need to do is establish urgency for the product you sell. You must establish a reason for the prospects to do business with you tonight—a reason that is believable, conceivable, and the truth.

If you sell a custom-made product, you can easily set up urgency. One of the easiest ways to put the point across to prospects is to say:

Mr. and Mrs. Prospect, we have talked a lot about your problems. Let me tell you a little about our problems as a custom manufacturer. Everything we do is predicated on an influx of orders coming into the manufacturing plant. We do not have the facilities to stockpile our product. You see, Mr. and Mrs. Prospect, we can't call our manufacturing facility and say, "Do you happen to have our product in a certain size or the color green?" because everything we manufacture is custom made.

Let's just assume, for the sake of conversation, that from all the sales representatives we have in the field, no orders come into the manufacturing facility for production. And the plant is like a big baby: when we don't feed it, it will start to cry. When it cries, we have two choices to make. We can either let key individuals stand around idle and pay them anyway, or we can lay them off. We choose the first option, because if we lay them off, they aren't going to wait around for us to call them back. They will seek other employment. And then when business picks up again, we have to train other employees, which costs us a ton of cash.

To alleviate this problem, we have found it a lot less expensive to offer significant savings to potential prospects who are in a position to take advantage of what we have to offer on the first night.

You can continue with this by saying:

You see, Mr. and Mrs. Prospect, we already know what the cost of raw materials is to produce our product, because we do stockpile parts and pieces. Unfortunately, though, we don't know what these materials will cost when we go back to reorder.

I wish I could call up the people who make the raw material and beg them not to increase prices. I wish I could call the people who sell us the paint, or the aluminum, and ask them not to increase prices. I wish I could ask all the laborers on the line not to take a cost of living increase, and the truck drivers who carry our product not to take a raise in salary because the cost of fuel has gone up. Mr. and Mrs. Prospect, the truth of the situation is, I can't do that.

Two things happen for those who wait, and both of them are bad. One, you continue to have the same problem you have today, and two, the price continues to go up. Mr. and Mrs. Prospect, with this in mind, I'm going to quote you two prices. One price is good for one year, barring any unseen price increase, and the second price is for people who are in a position to take advantage of what I have to offer today. Please understand I can take a Yes or I can take a No, but the sad part of the whole situation is my plant can't run on Maybe. Fair enough?

Price Tempting

The previous example is only one way to set up for a first-call close. Sales representatives sometimes tell prospects up front:

> I'm going to offer you a price that's good for one year, barring any unforeseen price increases, and then I'm going to offer you a price that will tempt you! This price is for people who are in a position to take advantage of what I have to offer the first day I'm in their home. Fair enough?

This kind of setup is essential for the first-call close. Prospects can make a decision on the first call if your company is reputable and your product is superb. They have to understand that if they want your product at the price you are quoting, they must sign on the dotted line. We are not trying to force them into signing, but we are attempting to sell our product to the exclusion of all other products out there. How do we do that if we don't ask for the order? Again, we must use a systematic approach when we ask for the order.

Asking prospects the question about price is very important. Let's try it again. "Would there be any reason, other than price, why we can't get together on an order for my product today?"

What are they going to say except "*Yes*," aside from "We want to get other prices. You are the first person we have seen!"?

This response, though, is bad news. If prospects want to get other prices, you must not have done your job to sell your product to the exclusion of all other products out there. The product demonstration that was filled with the mini-commitments apparently failed you.

Getting the shop-around excuse represents a definite flaw in the sales representative's presentation. Give me an "I don't think I can afford your product," and I will high-five all day long. I had to do a great job of price conditioning to get that response. Or if I get "We don't make a major decision like this on the first night," at least I can work with this objection and still close.

Halt the Stall

When they're facing the closing situation, some salespeople hate postponement. I particularly love this stall because I feel it is relatively easy to overcome. I simply say:

> Mr. and Mrs. Prospect, I respect the fact that you want to think about it. I guess the two things you need to think about are the money and terms, not whether or not you want the product, because I'm sure you do. When do you think you will be thinking about it?

The prospects answer, "Monday."

You say, "That's great! Let me ask you one question, Mr. and Mrs. Prospect. What's really going to change between now and Monday? I can answer that—only the price!"

At least this process will bring about much more informative dialogue between you and the prospects than the response "We want to get other estimates" will. If you spend two hours going through a presentation, and then prospects tell you they want to get other estimates, you should be flogged. (That response is one of my pet peeves that I work so hard not to hear at the end of the presentation or any place in between).

When prospects brings up an objection or stall, you should first make sure you understand what they are saying. Statements such as "Could you run that by me again?" or "I'm not sure I understand exactly what you meant," or "Could you be a little more specific? I'm not sure I'm following what you mean," are very important because they give prospects a chance to restructure or repeat what they said. They also give you a chance to regroup and regain composure so you can proceed with the sales presentation in a positive manner.

Keep Control

We all say things that come out wrong when we don't have a second chance to take back or restate what we've said. You can control the selling situation, however, by controlling the interaction, allowing prospects to reiterate what they might have communicated incorrectly, and giving them a second chance to clarify their previous statements.

As I've emphasized throughout this book, your goal is to keep control of the selling situation from start to finish. You do this by inserting words and statements into the presentation whenever you feel they are necessary. The statements are generally set-up lines you use to guide you from one step to another. For instance, before you quote the retail selling price, the statement you will make is:

> Mr. and Mrs. Prospect, I'm about to quote your total investment for this job. Before I do, I want you to understand that you have two ways to pay for the job. The first option is cash, which means one-third of the cost as a down payment, with the balance due upon satisfactory delivery of our product. The second option is installment payments, in which you pay nothing down and your first payment is due 30 days after satisfactory delivery of the product.

The statement is an explanation of exactly how prospects can pay for the product.

Buying Signs

It is important to recognize buying signs during the pre-close . These are things that prospects ask you, such as, "If we were to do this, when could we expect delivery?" or "Does your product come in any other colors?" or "Do you have financing available?" Again, remember that the ABCs of selling are to Always Be Closing. Don't rush to close, however, if the prospects give you some buying signs. Be patient, and ask questions such as, "When would you want delivery?" or "What color would you want it in?" or "If you were to do buy, would financing be important to you?" When prospects ask you a closing question, come back with a question.

Be Nice Till You Quote the Price

Remember: this does not mean to become obnoxious or rude. But it is definitely time to become serious about why you are in the prospects' house. You are there to close them. It's time to forget about the jokes and other conversation that detract from the closing sequence.

Box 'em In

Keep the conversation moving toward the close, and make absolutely sure that all doors have been closed. You see, the close is like a large room with a number of doors in it. The doors represent trap doors, and your job is to make sure that all the doors are closed, to box prospects in so they have no escape. If you move to close too quickly, there will always be an escape route for prospects to use. Pre-close is really the step at which you can move ahead as you gather strength toward the close (or be blown out of the water and forced to pack it up and move toward the door with your tail between your legs).

Present It, Seriously

"Be nice till you quote the price" does not mean you become a blazing idiot or a jerk. It just means that you need to be serious about what you are doing when it comes time to lay out that retail price. No more jokes or playing around; you must become focused on closing the sale. Many things will be going on simultaneously, and if you expect someone to give serious consideration to whether or not they should invest in your product, then you must be serious about how you present it.

Quoting the price means that you must give a complete breakdown that includes exactly what you intend to supply with prospects' purchase of your product. In a nutshell, this means to sum up the product. You need to list every feature, advantage, and benefit that prospects will derive from your product. You again need to do a complete product breakdown and make sure prospects understand exactly what they are getting for their hard-earned money.

You need to do this to build value into the price. For example, how do you sell a product for a $1,000? You make it worth $1,400. How do you make it worth $1,400? Remember: you justify the price by selling each piece as an independent unit. Then and only then can you go to close, which brings us back to quoting the retail selling *value*.

Lottery Game

To get an idea of where I am in pricing, one thing I like to say to prospects is this:

> Before I quote you the retail price, we are going to play a little game that is called the Homeview [name your company here] Lottery Game. You can't win anything, but I just want to see how well I did. Please, Mr. and Mrs. Prospect, write down separately on this little piece of paper what you think this product costs—not what you would like to pay. I just want to see how well I explained my product. I will not look at what you wrote down till after I have quoted our retail price. Fair enough?

After you quote your price, you will be able to look at the prospects' sheets, which tell you what they think they should pay. And then you merely sell the difference between their numbers and your price. As we've discussed, selling the difference between what they were willing to pay and the actual value of the product is much easier than attempting to sell the entire product price.

I don't know about you, but I really am not up for a cat-and-mouse game when it comes to quoting product price. Your goal should be to work your way to the point at which you can get the retail price out on the table for discussion. Then hold on to that price (and don't even consider lowering it) at least until you have justified why your product costs what it costs. No matter how long this justification takes, you must do it. If you rush to discount and quickly quote

Remember: Sell the Retail Price, but Not at Retail Price
Have prospects agree that your product is worth retail, and you have succeeded in your mission.

the price, the product will have lost tremendous value. Prospects also will believe that since you dropped your price once, you will do it repeatedly.

Reel the Deal

There is a bit of larceny in each and every one of us. If you hold onto the retail selling price, justify it, and appeal to the prospects' larceny, they will be more likely to invest in your product. Prospects want good deals—everybody wants good deals. Prospects want to be able to talk about their good deal to their friends, family, and relatives. They want to say, "Boy, did I get a great deal on this product!" They also want to say they beat the sales representative up, so to speak, to get the great deal.

You can accomplish this outcome only if you sell the *value* of the retail price, but not actually *at* the retail price. You must sell the worth of the product at retail. Then, and only then, do you have the right to discount the price.

Personally, I would never buy a product at retail, and I would never sell a product at retail. So if prospects decide to buy at retail, give something else away to them—something that is valued at what you would have discounted the product for. (I will not take advantage of people, nor will anyone else who works as a sales representative for me. If anyone on my sales force takes advantage of a prospect even one time, he or she doesn't work any more for our company.)

You don't need business based on deception. If you start highballing and lowballing prospects on your product, it won't be too long before you will be blackballed from the neighborhood. Always remember that people talk to each other, and they usually don't have a problem divulging what they paid for a product. When prospects talk and find out they paid a lot more than their friend for the same product . . . Well, you can imagine what will happen.

Getting to this point in your sales plan with prospects is a long process, but it's where you need to be to go to close. Remember, the close is the natural conclusion to the selling process.

What Do You Think?

In the pre-close, which is the set up for the closing sequence, it's important to have the commitments taken care of and already packaged in a nice little bundle, ready to deliver to the prospect. For example, one prospect occasionally will try to "throw the other prospect under the bus" by saying, "What do you think, Honey?" I shut this type of dialogue down immediately by saying to that prospect, "Let me ask you a question. If it's OK with her, is it going to be OK with you?" We just reversed the question and put it back where it belongs, in the hands of the person who asked it.

Body Language Speaks Loudly

Again, remember that enthusiasm is contagious, and you need to use it wisely to bring closure to the selling presentation. One way to tell whether your enthusiasm is effective is to "read" your prospects. As you go through the trials and tribulations of the pre-close, you can always tell where you are with prospects by reading their body language. Become familiar with body-language behaviors, and you can interrupt your presentation at any point to get things back on track and move toward a successful close.

Body Language Behaviors:

- **Boredom and Disinterest**

  Closing eyes while pinching bridge of nose with thumb and finger.

  Chewing or biting lip

  Moving eyes sideways

  Looking concerned or puzzled, with slight tilt of head

- **Confusion**

  Making unwavering eye contact, with right eye squinted, and right nostril raised and larger than left nostril

  Opening mouth at right side, and raising upper lip

  Placing hands on hips or in pocket with thumbs exposed

- **Enthusiasm and Understanding**

  Unable to maintain proper eye contact with you

  Blinking eyes while wide open

  Tapping one or both legs

  Placing hands in front of body, possibly on lap, and clasping them together

- **Evaluation**

  Folding arms across chest

  Squinting eyes

  Adjusting collar with fingers

  Scowling

  Angling body to speaker

- **Nervousness**

  Smiling

  Nodding affirmatively

  Leaning forward

  Maintaining eye contact

- **Power and Superiority**

  Frowning

  Scratching head

  Staring vacantly

  Avoiding eye contact

● **Skepticism**

Placing hand on or stroking chin

Tilting head slightly

Placing index finger on lips, or eyeglasses or pen in mouth

Turning ear toward speaker

● **Suspicion or Dishonesty**

Avoiding eye contact

Glancing sideways

Placing hands near or touching nose, ears, or mouth while
   speaking

Making gestures that don't match words

Poising body to move away

● **Uncertainty or Indecision**

Staring into space

Jingling objects in pocket or hands

Looking at watch

Picking at or adjusting clothing

Tapping or jiggling foot

When you have successfully pre-closed your prospects, the path is
clear for you to move forward toward the concluding steps of your
sales plan. When you reach this point in the process, you sense
from prospects' body language and possibly even their comments
that it's time to go for the close.

STEP 8

Close

- Create Urgency

- Close All Trap Doors

- Narrow It Down to Price and Terms

- Overcome All Stall and Excuses

- Box Them Up

- Use Open Ended Questions

- Elicit Yes Responses

- Don't Give Up

- Draft Contract

- Assume the Sale

I operate under the assumption that silence means consent. If you have no response from prospects for a lengthy period of time, assume the silence as a go-ahead with the sale. Then extend your hand to them and say, "Thank you so much for putting your trust and confidence in me. I promise I won't let you down. You certainly made a wise investment. Congratulations, and thank you for your business!"

The assumptive close also means pulling a contract and starting to write. If the prospects don't say a word, again assume their silence as a go-ahead for the sale. Far too many sales representatives fear pulling a contract and beginning to write. By far, this is the hardest thing to teach a new sales representative to do. Just realize that the worst thing that can happen if you pull the contract is that the prospects will ask, "What are you doing?"

If this happens, you simply reply, "I'm writing up the contract."

They then will inform you, "We're not ready to do this now."

Your come back with, "I'm sorry, I misunderstood. I thought this was something you wanted to go ahead with! When do you think you will be ready to do so?"

At least with this interaction, you know where you are in the sales presentation. Do not under any circumstances take the prospects' response as a "No, we are not buying!" It simply means you're ready to start closing the sale using closing tactics, which I will present to

SALES PRO TIP

Objection Does Not Mean Rejection
Do not, under any circumstance, read **objection** as **rejection**! Take the word **objection** out of your sales vocabulary. Instead, refer to objections as stalls, or as slight bumps in the road. Take no offense to prospects using a stall. A stall simply means you have not given them enough information from which to make a true decision about whether or not they want to buy your product. It's a good thing when prospects show enough interest to let you try to close them.

you. The goal of these closing tactics is to help bring your selling situation to a successful conclusion.

And remember that salespeople who feel rejected by the constant barrage of stalls will not be able to close the sale. They will be intimidated and have a tendency to shy away from the close.

Ferret Out the Reasons

If prospects have not been persuaded to move ahead on the investment in your product, their delay might be for any of a variety of reasons. You just need to ferret out the real reason and go from there. Here are some of the most common arguments you'll hear:

- **"The price is too high! Too much money!"**
  (*Your response*) "Mr. and Mrs. Prospect, I know it's a lot, but isn't it your experience that it's better to spend a little more than you'd planned than a little less than you should?"

- **"I'm not ready right now!"**
  (*Your response*) "Mr. and Mrs. Prospect, it's a natural thing to want to put off a major decision, but let me share what some of my "happiest" customers have told me. They have told me they were concerned at first, but now that the product is working, they are sure glad they didn't wait and lose that discount."

- **"I want to check other prices; I'll get back to you."**
  (*Your response*) "Mr. and Mrs. Prospect, just to clarify my own thinking . . . There are three elements in making a good decision, and you have a question on just one of those elements, the price. What about the second element, the company, or the third element, the product?"

- **"I want to think it over; leave your card."**
  (*Your response*) "Mr. and Mrs. Prospect, if you weren't serious about investing in my product, you wouldn't waste time wanting to thinking it over, would you? You would just say No, wouldn't you? Let me just be sure of this—you did like my product, didn't you?"

- **"I don't like high-pressure sales tactics."**

  (Your response) "Mr. and Mrs. Prospect, if you were my best friend, and I was telling you about something that could literally save you thousands of dollars, would you consider that pressure? I'm sorry if I came across a little strong, but it's because I have tremendous belief in my product and company. Can you forgive me?"

- **"I want to discuss it with my son/daughter/parents."**

  (Your response) "Mr. and Mrs. Prospect, I'm glad you want to discuss this with your son or daughter because that means you are sincerely interested in my product, or there would not be nothing to discuss. My experience with sons and daughters is that they are all cut from the same mold. If you see value, so will they. But because it's you who will be getting the benefit of the value, it really is your decision, isn't it?"

- **"I want to check out your company."**

  (Your response) "Mr. and Mrs. Prospect, that's a curious statement. One thing that is usually quite obvious to people is the strength and integrity of our company. However, this is no problem. Let me review the things you should check."

- **"I don't make a decision like this in one night."**

  (Your response) "Mr. and Mrs. Prospect, I understand. I have a feeling that the reason we can't get together is not that you can't make a decision but that you want to be sure you are making the right decision. Is that correct?"

- **"The payment is too high."**

  (Your response) "Mr. and Mrs. Prospect, I understand. You feel the monthly payment is too high. Let me understand clearly. If one way or another I could get that monthly obligation more in line with something you can afford, you would make a decision to go ahead with my product, wouldn't you?"

● **"I have lived a long time without your product; why do I need it now?"**

(Your response) "Mr. and Mrs. Prospect, you are at a point in your life where things should be getting easier for you, not harder. Wouldn't you agree?"

● **"I don't use financing. I'll wait until I can pay cash."**

(Your response) "Mr. and Mrs. Prospect, it's cheaper to absorb interest rates than it is a cost-of-living escalation. Here, let me show you."

● **"I won't make a down payment. I'll pay on completion only."**

(Your response) "Mr. and Mrs. Prospect, we do have a way to do this. Let me explain. What I can do is write it up as 90 days the same as cash, and when the product is delivered, you will pay in full and the application and the loan are tossed into the garbage can. Sound fair?"

● **"I'll sign, but I have three days to cancel, don't I?"**

(Your response) "Mr. and Mrs. Prospect, of course you do. But if you have plans to cancel, please let's not bother with the paperwork. If I may ask, what part of this proposal is it that might give you a reason to cancel the contract?"

● **"The interest is too high; I won't pay those rates."**

(Your response) "Mr. and Mrs. Prospect, our rates actually are just about as good as they come. We pass millions of dollars through this bank, and our customers get a preferred rate. Let me break it down for you."

● **"I'm too old; let my heirs buy the product."**

(Your response) "I understand. It seems that many folks from your generation sometimes aren't comfortable doing nice things for themselves. Let's look at it from your heirs' point of view; they love you, don't they?"

● **"My employment is not secure."**

(Your response) "I understand. Many companies make their people feel like they are on the chopping block. But you can't stop living and caring for your family."

● **"We want to shop other products."**

(Your response) "Mr. and Mrs. Prospect, I'm confused. You did say that our product was the product you wanted, didn't you? What is it exactly that you want to shop for?"

● **"I want to talk to other people who have your product."**

(Your response) "Mr. and Mrs. Prospect, that's great, but let me make sure you are aware that whenever you ask for referrals, you don't think a company would give you any bad referrals, do you? A company will give you only people who it knows are satisfied with its product or service. You need to be satisfied with the product and service, and the only way you can do that is to have the company give you a 30-day, money-back guarantee. You are the best referral we can give you, and you will be completely satisfied."

● **"I have other priorities (tuition, car, roof, etc.)."**

(Your response) "Mr. and Mrs. Prospect, that makes you like most of us today, trying to lay claim to our income. Let me show you a way you can have both of these important things, and perhaps your total outlay will be even less than it is now. How does that sound to you?"

● **"I had a bad experience with another company."**

(Your response) "I understand, Mr. and Mrs. Prospect, that you have been burned before by what you considered to be a quick decision. Unfortunately, many of us have found ourselves in the same position and have had a similar experience. The sad thing is that about 5 percent of the business world consists of con men. And the other sad part is that person who conned you has taken control of your life; and unfortunately, he or she has thrown you into the constant state of procrastination and will always have control over you if you let that happen. What I mean by that is you are living in the past, avoiding today, and ruining your tomorrow. How can you let that person continue to ruin your life by not acting on legitimate opportunities that are in the best interest of you and

your family? Always remember, it's not a question of when you deal, but with whom. Let's go ahead and do this, OK?"

I have given you one example rebuttal for handling each of the stalls above to give you start on what to say and how to handle each of them. Also, I would not classify any of the above statements as an objection.

The Art of Negotiating

The art of negotiating also plays an important part in closing the sale. Effective negotiation also requires a systematic approach. Let's have a look at the steps involved (and you'll recognize some of these steps because they've been introduced earlier in the book). How to Negotiate:

1. Always smile and be sincere, and stay in control of the selling situation.
2. Telegraph your statements; don't write letters. Ask open-ended questions, which prospects must respond to with more than a *Yes* or *No*.
3. Be a great listener. Don't just conveniently listen; make sure you hear what prospects say.
4. Be an attentive observer. Look and carefully analyze what the prospects are showing you through their body language.
5. Try not to interpret what prospects say, but pay close attention and be very attentive to what they mean.
6. All prospects will try to convince you they have great knowledge about your product, and they will try to hurry you along. Do not let these attempts vary your presentation in any way, and do not let prospects convince you to short-cut the presentation.
7. Prospects who have a fear of buying might turn gruff, or begin joking and laughing, or become non-attentive, or attempt to take charge of the selling situation. Do not let these efforts rattle you; just stay the course.

8. Always remember that the female controls the spending of money 80 percent of the time, and the male dominates the conversation 80 percent of the time.

9. I have grown up in an environment in which "Yes, sir." and "No, sir," "Yes, ma'am," and "No, ma'am" are used. I'm not a firm believer in immediately trying to get on a first-name basis with prospects. I much prefer to address prospects as Mr. and Mrs. unless they are emphatic that I address them by their first names. This represents what is called visitor protocol. Abide by it.

10. Be ready to address all prospect objections or stalls when it comes to the price presentation close. You must be ready to handle these knee-jerk comments and move on as quickly as possible.

11. "Save that till they say that." In other words, don't put words in prospects' mouths by telling them what they feel. Let them tell you what they feel, even if your empathy level pushes you in the other direction.

12. Get your major or minor commitments before you attempt to close. If you don't do this, you might compromise the sale.

Give Prospects Reasons to Buy

Prospects today are well informed about how to negotiate a better price. Whether it's a car dealer, a flea market, a garage sale, or a trip to Mexico, prospects are well versed in the art of negotiation. My son is fifteen, and even at the retail store he speaks to the manager to see whether he can get a better price (maybe he got this from me!).

People buy when they have been given a reason to buy, and not until then. You must be able to substantiate both the price of your product and—even more so—the reason for a discount if you offer one. If both are not believable, desirable, and factual, you can forget about walking away with an order.

Commitment Close

When you feel the time is right, you should move to a trial close. Trial closes involve statements such as "If I could . . . , would you?" This is an example of what we refer to as a *commitment close*.

Also, ask simple, responsive, reflex questions such as "What is your middle initial?" or "What is your house address?" or "Let me get the correct spelling of your last name." These are all part of the assumptive close.

An *alternate-choice close* should play an important role for the new and the old sales representative. An example of the alternate-choice close might be as simple as "Mr. and Mrs. Prospect, the product comes in brown and white; which would you prefer?" or "Mr. and Mrs. Prospect, the payment is $122 for 36 months or $101 for 48 months; which of these fits better into your budget?" Start writing the contract based on prospects' answer to this alternate-choice question.

High Down Payment and High Monthly Obligation

Another close I like to use is *high down payment and a high monthly obligation*. It goes like this:

> Mr. and Mrs. Prospect, the total cost of the investment is $12,425 (say the thousands, hundreds, dollars and cents). Now if you are in a position to take advantage of what I have to offer today, I can do it for $9,300 (say "ninety-three hundred"). That would be $4,000 (say "four thousand dollars") down, and with financing, $5,300 (say "five thousand three hundred dollars") for 12 months, at $468.39 (say "four hundred sixty-eight dollars and thirty-nine cents") a month.

After you quote the price, shut up.

Finally, the prospects might say, "That's too much."

Your rebuttal is "What's too much, the down payment or the monthly obligation?"

They answer, "Both."

You respond, "Let's see if I understand this correctly. If the monthly obligation and the down payment were something you could afford, then this is something you would go ahead and do?"

The prospects answer, "Yes!"

Done deal. All you need to do is make it affordable.

Let's say the prospects say, "The down payment is too much."

You again say, "So it's the down payment is it? Let me ask you a question. I'm not saying I can, but let's just assume that I was able to greatly reduce the amount of money you need down. Then is this something we could go ahead with?"

By quoting a high down and a high monthly obligation, you have taken their mind off all the other objections and stalls that they may have in store for you and brought the decision point down to where it should be—price and terms. And negotiating these are much easier than negotiating any other type of objection or stall.

Note how I quoted the price to the prospects. I quoted the first price, which would have been the retail price, in thousands, hundreds, dollars, and cents. You'll want to say it very slowly, and let it sink in. I quoted the second price only in hundreds. Saying "ninety three hundred" sounds much better than saying "nine thousand, three hundred dollars." You'll use the first price to emphasize the amount of money that it would cost without a discount. You want

SALES PRO TIP

Sales Without Profits—the Fool's Dream
Don't fall into the trap of being a leader in sales at all costs, even if that means selling without a profit.

this price to hit home and sound like a tremendous amount of money.

Word Interpretation

You also want to pay close attention to how you phrase your words, not only in the close, but throughout the sales presentation. Words can be interpreted to mean a variety of different things, depending even on such a subtle thing as your inflection, or where you put the emphasis when you speak them. Here's an example of one sentence that, depending on how you say it, can mean seven different things. As you say each sentence, emphasize the word in bold.

1. **I** did not say he beat his wife!
   This means you are not the one who said he beat his wife.
2. I **did not** say he beat his wife!
   This means you didn't make this statement at all.
3. I did not **say** he beat his wife!
   This means you implied he beat his wife without explicitly saying so.
4. I did not say **he** beat his wife!
   This means someone else beat his wife.
5. I did not say he **beat** his wife!
   This means he did something else to her.
6. I did not say he beat **his** wife!
   This means he beat someone else's wife.
7. I did not say he beat his **wife**!
   This means he beat something else other than his wife—maybe his child or girlfriend.

As you can see, the sentence takes on seven different meanings based on the words that you emphasize. Similarly, your prospects might incorrectly interpret your conversation if you mistakenly emphasize the wrong word. They can easily misinterpret what is said, and based on their misinterpretation, formulate an opinion that causes them to make an incorrect decision about whether they should or should not purchase your product.

Hang Around, Warm Down

Whenever you break bread with your customers—which is what you're doing when you're selling a contract, never eat and run. When you have closed the sale, put all your stuff away and talk about anything except what the prospects just purchased. Talk about their families, or their children, or anything they want to talk about. Your words must be sincere and come naturally; people can read a phony person.

And relax your prospects by communicating in a calm voice. Toward the end of the conversation, ask them whether they feel comfortable with their purchase. They will be more relaxed by this time and will divulge their true feelings about the purchase they have made.

Warm Down

One of the laws of sales is "After all is said and done, usually more is said than done!" That is why you need to hang around and warm down, to make sure all the prospects' questions are answered.

If the prospects continue to say No, you have a better chance to close if you put them at ease. You can put them at east by beginning to put your stuff away. When they see you doing that, they think you are done and will begin to relax.

When they are totally relaxed, ask them this question: "Mr. and Mrs. Prospect, do you think you will ever buy this product from anyone?"

Wait for their answer, which should be *Yes*.

Then proceed, "What do I have to do to earn your business?" Again, wait for a response. Regardless of their answer, follow it with:

> Look, Mr. and Mrs. Prospect, I need your business, I want your business, and I will do anything to get your business, even if it means discounting the price. I think you people can get me a lot of business, and I'm willing to do something special for you to make this happen. Believe me, when I say discount, I'm not talking nickels and dimes, but a huge chunk of change."

Then, follow up with:

> Mr. and Mrs. Prospect, this is not something I do on a regular basis. The only thing I would ask of you is that, if you decided to do this, you agree to complete confidentiality. I'm sure what you pay for things is your business and not anyone else's business. I can't sell my product to anyone else at the price I am about to sell it to you for. If anyone asks you what you paid, I don't care if you say you paid more, but please don't tell other people what you really paid. Fair enough?

And then you follow up with the discounted price. Setting up the close in this way will be useful because the prospects are relaxed, and instead of trying to "nice you out of the house" (get rid of you in a nice way), they are faced with a *Yes* or *No* response.

Relieve Them From the Silence

At this point, prospects' thinking becomes much clearer because they are thinking about only one thing, and that is whether or not they should go ahead with the investment in your product. You might have to bring price justification back into this closing scenario, but you should just wait it out to see. Once you throw out a close, wait for a response from the prospects. A standard rule is that in a closing situation, after you have asked a closing question, you should shut up. The principle is that the first one who talks loses. But I don't believe this, because prospects can freeze in a closing situation.

Freezing means prospects don't want to say *No* and they don't want to say *Yes*, so they say nothing. This pause can last a long time, and the silence is enough to drive you stark-raving mad. It's time to intercede, or the prospects might fly off the handle because the silence also is upsetting to them. If you wait for them to respond, their reaction might well be to finally say, "We are not ready to make this decision; please pack your stuff and get out!" This is not the response you are looking for. In fact, you want to do everything in your power to keep it from happening. In this case, silence is not golden; it's detrimental.

If the prospects don't respond, you must relieve them of the silence and say something like

> Mr. and Mrs. Prospect, I know this is a tough decision, and I want you to be comfortable with any decision you make. Give me 10 percent of your trust, and let me earn the other 90 percent. What do you say?

This strategy is called *stimulating the close* with a *counter close*. And if that doesn't work, you will move to the *counter* of the counter close:

> Mr. and Mrs. Prospect; I want your business whenever you are ready to do business. You two are mature adults and can make a decision without my influence. The only thing I really want to say is that if anyone ever had a genuine need for my product, it's you folks. Please don't deprive yourself of the opportunity to own it at the price I quoted you. Just remember, Mr. and Mrs. Prospect, long after you've forgotten the price, the quality of the product will live on. Let's do this, OK?

Doorknob Close

Even as you walk toward the door, you still have a few more closes that you can attempt. The doorknob close is designed for when you are walking out of the prospects' house. Remember—this is one of the only times you will find prospects totally relaxed throughout the entire sales presentation because you are giving them the illusion that you are leaving their home.

They don't realize you are about to go right back into a close when you ask them, "Mr. and Mrs. Prospect, now that I'm leaving, can you answer one simple question?"

They will answer, "*Yes.*"

In turn, you will say:

> I'm leaving, and I really thought we were going to get together, but the problems you had before I arrived will still remain. I'm sure you are aware of the tremendous need you have for my product or a product just like ours. Is that correct?

They will answer, "*Yes.*" (Note that if their answer is No, it's time to beat feet and get out of there. Remember to say "NEXT!" to yourself in this situation, and begin focusing right now on the next prospects, the next presentation.)

To their positive response, you will say, "Just so I can clear this up in my mind, let's say someone else comes in and shows you a product. This product can do everything my product can do, is made of the same material as my product, functions the same as my product but is offered at a much lower in price. You would go ahead and buy this other product—am I right in this assumption?"

They say, "*Yes!*"

Follow their response with, "Let me ask you another question then. If I laid three stones resembling diamonds in front of you, and one was a real diamond and the other two were imitations, could you tell them apart?"

They answer, "*No.*"

Your response then will be:

> There is an old saying that goes "If you don't know your diamonds, then you'd better know your jeweler." Products like ours bear the same traits. Let's say I lay three products out in front of you. They could weigh the same, function the same, and look exactly alike, yet one could be different from the others in virtually a hundred ways. You have given me a good indication that it's just the price that's keeping us apart. Let me see what I can work out. May I use your phone?

You must go to the phone to discount the price, because if you can discount it on your own at this point, the prospects will lose all faith in you and your company. And you must have a valid basis for using third-party influence to discount the price now. A reduction in price here must include some sort of trade off. For instance, you might ask your company to advance some of your anticipated referral fees to the prospects so you can offer a better up-front price. In other words, you might ask your company for a discount based on the number of potential people these prospects can supply to you as leads through networking with their coworkers, friends, and family. Whatever reason you use, you and your company must have agreed upon it so you can use it in this situation. You must not discount the order or lower the price arbitrarily for prospects to take advantage of your product.

Practice Makes Perfect

Once again, the scenarios I've described are setups for a closing situation that falls under confidence selling. You must have control of the close, and established lines are extremely important. Just as a magician uses chatter to convince his audience of an illusion, you too must set up with words what you can do for the prospect. You will memorize the chatter you use, so it will flow when you use it. Accomplishing this involves lots of practice with key lines. Do this practice in a car with a tape recorder, or at home in front of a mirror, or in front of family members. Practice does make perfect, and the more the dialogue flows, the better chance you have to close the sell.

As you're probably noticing, there are many closing techniques, and I would need more than just this book to cover them all. I do want to stir your imagination, however, and provide you with several options that you can use when you're placed in what seem to be dead-end situations. So let's say you have reached your wit's end and have no place else to go. At that point, try this:

> Mr. and Mrs. Prospect, I feel badly that I couldn't help you out here tonight. Let me get my stuff together and get out of you hair. The reason I feel a little hesitant to leave is because tomorrow my boss will ask me what happened on this call tonight. He will ask, "Did the folks like the product? Did you high-pressure them? Is that why they didn't invest? Will the product do them some good? Did you offer them the bonus savings plan? Then why didn't they buy?" Every one of these questions will be addressed to me because you won't be there. What should I tell him?

The goal of this close is to get the real objection or stall out on the table again. You have given yourself another opportunity to attack the real problem.

Closing also sometimes involves third-party influence. Using third-party influence to support your product is great, but when prospects want to draw on third-party influence as a objection or a stall, you need to nip that in the bud by saying the following (yes, I used this example earlier, but it's worth repeating):

> Mr. and Mrs. Prospect, I'm glad you want to talk to a third party, because that tells me you are really interested in my product or there would be nothing to talk about, would there? When you do talk to the third party, I'm sure you realize only four things could possibly happen. Let's look at these four and only four options. If you said *Yes* and the third party said *Yes*, then the answer would be *Yes*, correct? Now if you say *No*, and they say *No*, then the answer would be No, correct again? If you said *No*, I don't want this product, and they said *Yes*, you should have it, the answer would be No. Is this in fact the case? If you said *Yes*, I really want the product, and they said No, I don't think it's a good idea, but you really wanted the product, the answer would be *Yes*. I'm going to assume that would be correct, true? So would you agree with me that contrary to what the third party says, it still breaks down that the final decision is yours and yours alone? Wouldn't you agree? Let's go ahead and do this, OK?

Third-party influence can be an asset if you close the sale using the above close. Each and every time you go to close you learn some new way to handle an objection or a stall. This is why learning the sales game takes time. Don't be quick to give up if the solution doesn't come to you immediately. Good things come to those who wait, and don't ever forget that.

Hang in There

If you give two presentations a day and give them 300 days a year, you will have given 600 presentations in one year. You will have been involved in 600 closes. You will have heard the same stalls and learned how to handle each one a little differently. In short, you will gain a vast amount of knowledge if you just hang in there.

What you can do with your mind is endless. Learn to use it wisely by keeping it positive. Never allow negativity to enter into it (nobody has the right to put trash your mind—that's what dumps are for). Your mind is just like a computer, garbage in, garbage out. So surround yourself with successful people. Positive thinking yields positive results.

Relieve the Pressure

Always relieve the pressure in a selling situation by using a respect-ful line such as "I can appreciate what you are saying." You should always use this approach when you're moving into the close. Think how you feel when people agree with you. Agreement seems to put prospects' minds at ease. Follow this comment with "Mr. and Mrs. Prospect, obviously you would not take your valuable time to think this over if you were not interested. Is that correct?" This is an important question to use in any type of stall prospects might throw at you that indicates their indecision.

Another line you might want to use to ferret out the true stall is "Mr. and Mrs. Prospect, you're not saying that just to get rid of me are you?" You're back into the closing sequence as you state, "That's good. Maybe you can answer something here to help me in the future. Did I say or do anything to offend you?" Follow this with "I feel so relieved. Do you feel comfortable with my product and company?" And then, "Does my product have everything you would want and need in a product, or does it have more than you want?" Follow up again with "Is the monthly obligation something that is affordable to you?" Follow that with "Is it when the monthly obliga-tion starts or the total investment price?"

Reduce to Ridiculous

Following this closing sequence keeps prospects talking and still gives you the opportunity to reduce the investment to the ridicu-lous. Let's review this concept presented earlier with a different example:

- Divide the total investment by 10 years. Let us assume the investment is $9,000; $9,000 divided by 10 equals $900 a year for a 10-year period.

- Next, divide $900 by 12 months to get the monthly expendi-ture, which is $75.

- Next, divide the $75 per month by 30 days, which is $2.50 a day.

- Next, divide $2.50 per day by the 24 hours in a day, which results in slightly more than 10 cents an hour. Who couldn't afford 10 cents an hour?

That is how you break down the investment to the ridiculous, so prospects understand that it is within reach of their budget.

Often, prospects have received a lower estimate for a product that is not as good as your product—maybe the other product doesn't have the same warranty as yours, for example. So prospects are not really comparing apples to apples. You need to address this situation by saying:

> Mr. and Mrs. Prospect, in today's busy marketplace, the laws of consumerism prohibit people from paying just a little and receiving a lot. With inflation as it is, and prices constantly on the upswing, and given the premise that price buyers are twice buyers, you will spend twice as much on the other product by having to buy again another time. You don't want to waste your money, do you? Let's do it right, OK?

Lines that ring true in this regard are "The bitterness of poor quality remains long after the sweetness of the low price is forgotten."

If you follow the steps and processes outlined throughout this chapter, you can begin to feel confident of your ability to close successfully on at least one-third of your presentations. And depending on how many additional *Yes* answers you can inspire from prospects, your close rate can quickly climb toward the 50 percent mark.

Post-Close

- **Reassure**

- **Present the Future**

- **Confront the Situation**

- **Be Realistic**

- **Address Further Concerns**

- **Ask for Leads**

- **Warm Down**

- **Don't Overstay Your Welcome**

Post-Close

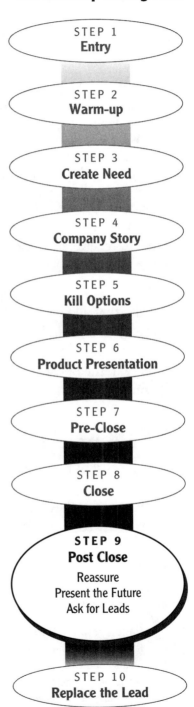

The Ten Step Selling Plan

STEP 1
Entry

STEP 2
Warm-up

STEP 3
Create Need

STEP 4
Company Story

STEP 5
Kill Options

STEP 6
Product Presentation

STEP 7
Pre-Close

STEP 8
Close

STEP 9
Post Close
Reassure
Present the Future
Ask for Leads

STEP 10
Replace the Lead

The post-close is an essential part of the selling plan for you to PYI (Protect Your Income). Effectively handling the post-close phase of selling means being aware of and knowing how to deal with several possible scenarios that you might encounter with prospects, even after they've decided to buy your product and signed on the dotted line.

Battling Buyer's Remorse

A lot has transpired from the time of your arrival in the prospects' home to your now-pending time of departure. So many sales representatives "eat and run" (get the sale and get out), only to find that the impending doom—the sales cancellation—beats them back to the office.

So many times after I have left a sales presentation feeling good about the sale, I arrive at the office the next morning and receive a phone call

Take Phone Calls with a Positive Voice
When you receive a phone call from prospects the day after the sale, train your mind to think they want to add product, not that they want to rescind the contract. When you pick up the phone and have this mindset, prospects read a positive attitude in your voice.

from the people I closed. They say they didn't sleep all night and wish to cancel the contract. This phone call is one of the hardest for me to receive, because it tells me I didn't do my job with them in the post-close.

When I close a sale, the personal part of me is so happy to get the order that all I want to do is get out of the house before the buyers change their mind. But as I've matured in selling, I've learned that, if and when the buyers change their minds, I really want to be right there in the house in front of them, so I can handle the situation immediately.

Handle It in the House

When customers decide to cancel, getting back in their good graces is very difficult after you leave, whether the same day or the next day. Because they feel they have hurt your feelings, they are extremely reluctant to see you again after they have cancelled. You

Handle It in the House
Remember that any unresolved issues or questions clients might have about your product or their commitment to buy are much easier to address and resolve before you leave their home. Once you've walked out the door, getting back inside is sometimes not possible.

were a friend throughout the presentation, and now they have jeopardized that friendship. They have gone back on their word, and they feel badly about that. They make a subconscious decision not to want to see you, talk to you, or hear from you or your company ever again.

Customers who cancel on an order might even say bad things about you to other people to try to rationalize their own behavior. The sad part is they really don't want to hurt you, but doing so is their way to end the relationship and get out of the dilemma they put themselves in by purchasing something they no longer believe they want, need, or can afford.

These prospects are suffering from a severe case of *buyer's remorse*—one of the sickest diseases a prospect can get. And they can come down with it at a moment's notice. Buyer's remorse affects every part of their logical thinking processes and destroys their memory cells so they can't even remember why they signed the contract in the first place. All they know is that they want out. Every step of the sales presentation is gone from their mind, and the only thing they feel is regret.

No shots, pills, or antidotes exist to cure this frustrating disease of buyer's remorse. There are no cures, only preventative measures. You can "vaccinate" prospects ahead of time, during the post-close of your sales presentation, to let them know they might come down with buyer's remorse. And you can definitely head off buyer's remorse at the pass if you caution prospects that experiencing it is normal and natural.

Solidify the Order

Here is what you need to do as the sales representative, both to prepare prospects for, and to ward off, buyer's remorse. You must leave them some literature that describes their purchase, so that when they feel the remorse setting in they will have something to look at that brings them back to wanting the product. Here's what I say to prospects:

> Mr. and Mrs. Prospect, later, after I leave, you are going to go through something that is called buyer's remorse. This experience might be related to the money you will spend on the product, or what friends or relatives might think, or even just about whether or not you're doing the right thing by buying this product.
>
> First, I would like to be the first to congratulate you on a wise investment. You have had the chance to see all the features, advantages, and benefits of our product.
>
> This will be the only time you will hear someone congratulate you on your wise investment. Others who have not seen the demonstration will probably tell you are nuts for paying what you paid. They don't understand that this is an investment, not an expenditure, and that it will pay for itself in the near future.
>
> When you feel that you have made a wrong decision, look at the picture I'm leaving with you, and remember everything my product will do for you. Also remember that if I could wave a magic wand and let you experience the product right now, you would never, ever consider canceling. And you might have questions that pop up later after I leave, so please feel free to call me anytime. I will be there to answer any of your questions, day or night.
>
> Thank you again for your trust, and I assure you, you won't be sorry. You do feel all right about this investment, don't you?

Wait for their answer now, and handle it accordingly.

Right of Recission

In dealing with buyer's remorse, you need to keep in mind the federal *Right of Recission* ruling: buyers have the right to cancel the contract without any penalty or obligation within three business days of the date of the contract. That's also why you need to solidify the order in the post-close. Solidifying the order means making the prospects comfortable with their investment so they don't exercise their right of recission. When I present the Right of Recission regulation to prospects, I sometimes explain,

> This is the Right of Recission clause, which gives you three days to cancel the contract. Let me explain. A while back, some con men would high-pressure people into buying things, and buyers would be locked

into the contract even when they found out they were dealing with a fly-by-night organization. To prevent this from happening, the federal government passed a Right of Recission ruling to give the people time to check on the company and make sure it is reputable and honest. You do feel we are a reputable company, don't you, Mr. and Mrs. Prospect?

And add this line to your selling repertoire:

> Mr. and Mrs. Prospect, if you have any doubt about this investment, please sign where it says "I hereby cancel this contract." I pride myself on having zero cancellations, because the people I deal with understand exactly why they need my product, and they really start looking forward to owning it and having it delivered as soon as possible. I can't tell you how many orders I have had to put on rush because of people's excitement. I advise you as newfound friends: if you have any bad feelings, don't sign anything, and let's discuss it further.

This is a much better way to handle a potential sales cancellation and bring the matter to the forefront, so you can deal with it immediately.

One situation that might cause you to go back to square one is when prospects balk at signing the Right of Recission. You can see

SALES PRO TIP

Times Have Changed So Much

The selling game today has taken on an altogether different flavor from earlier times. Salespeople are generally highly educated, hard working, and honest. If they have been in business for any period of time, they are also highly service orientated. They believe their job is to please prospects, and they will do everything in their power to provide excellent service. Salespersons strongly believe that customers are always right and, if necessary, they will battle their own company to defend their customers.

Salespeople usually are family oriented and attend church regularly. Their faith is number one on their list of priorities.

Times have changed so much. It used to be that time was money, and money was time, but not anymore. Time is time, and more importantly, time is life. Use it honestly and wisely.

them cringe when you begin to explain the paperwork, and you can feel the recission coming on. People will do an exorbitant amount of thinking when it comes to putting their "John Henry" on a contract. All the stories they've ever heard about unscrupulous contractors come to mind, and they can easily panic. Your job is to rid prospects of this preconceived notion that all salespeople are crooks.

Why They May Cancel

People cancel their contract for a number of different reasons. Some cancel because they don't feel comfortable after you leave. The ether wears off, so to speak, and reality sets in. As I mentioned at the beginning of this book, some salespeople's positive mental attitude gives them the power to put prospects into a hypnotic trance, and this experience is completely out of the ordinary for them. The prospects are used to dealing with life in a negative environment, and you are such a breath of fresh air with your positive attitude that they become overwhelmed and let themselves be led down any road you wish to lead them.

Third-party influence is another reason for prospects to cancel on a sale. This third party could be a son or daughter, an aunt or uncle, a brother or sister, a neighbor or friend, another company, or even a stranger who advises them they are spending too much money when they approach him or her for a loan at the credit union. Everyone they talk to is an expert on the product they just invested in. They all say they could have gotten the prospects a better price, or they know someone who knows someone who could have gotten them a better deal.

As we discussed earlier, when people buy something, they are likely to tell other people, and all of these people have words of wisdom for your customers. And if your customers were at all concerned and confused before, they are now bewildered, and their reaction to this bewilderment is often to cancel the contract.

Future Pacing

Now that you understand what can transpire to cause customers to cancel on the sale, it's up to you to fend off all of these situations. You will use something called *future pacing* to help you solidify the sale. To future pace, you once again tell prospects exactly what might happen before it happens.

> Mr. and Mrs. Prospect, tomorrow when you wake up and go to work, you are going to tell a number of your friends that you invested in my product. And you are also going to tell them what you paid. Now the funny thing is, because they didn't see what you saw, every one of them might tell you that you spent too much money. The sad part is that you know far more than any of them who are giving you advice. You have been schooled on exactly what makes the product better than the rest—the features, advantages, and benefits of the product you invested in. You are comfortable with everything and have never been more educated about this kind of product. Is that correct? So what are you going to say to those people who want to give you advice?

Hopefully, your prospects will stop all their well-intentioned friends and family midstream and say, "I have researched this product, and I'm very comfortable with my decision." You see, you have given the prospects confidence to be able to avoid negative feedback from outside influence.

But this is not where your job ends. You must now proceed to the next phase by saying:

> Mr. and Mrs. Prospect, in every family I have ever come in contact with, there is always a naysayer—you know, a person who projects doom and gloom, a person who will tell you that you are crazy for spending that kind of money on this kind of product. Who among your family members or friends would that be?

They will think for a moment and say something like "Probably my brother. He is always telling me what I should do and shouldn't do."

You will follow this response with:

> So, Mr. and Mrs. Prospect, when your brother tells you that you made a bad decision, the way I see it, you have a couple alternatives.

> First, you could agree with him, even though he hasn't seen what the product will do for you as far as saving you time or money. Or second, you could remember all of the time we have spent going over everything that my product can and will do for you—which, by the way, your brother did not see.
>
> The most important thing is that you both know this is a true investment rather than an expenditure, and you feel very comfortable with that, don't you? With all of this in mind, what will you say to your brother when he tries to discourage you?

Wait for the answer, which I'm quite sure will be positive. But then again, even if it's not, you are still in the house to work things out.

Sometimes, if you have an uneasy feeling that prospects might be uncomfortable with their decision, you're wise to take something out to the car and let them spend some time alone to have a little powwow about their decision. Then, when you get back inside, you address the situation: "I'm sure while I was out you two had some time to openly discuss this between yourselves. Are you both still OK with your decision?"

Again, the worst thing that can happen is also the best thing that can happen. You have the opportunity to resell the prospects if the situation blows up in your face. At least you are still in the house to handle it. I can't emphasize enough the importance of being in the clients' home dealing with their concerns, rather than at the office with a recission in your hand, wondering why the prospects don't pick up the phone as you try to call them for the hundredth time.

SALES PRO TIP

Deal with It
Sometimes when I tell sales representatives that they had a recission, they don't act surprised at all. They make the incredible statement that "I knew they were going to cancel!" If they knew the prospects were going to cancel, wouldn't it have been easier to confront the situation and deal with it while they were in their home? If they knew so much, they would have wanted to protect their income.

People often also balk when they see the finance charge. Their key statement is always, "You said it was only going to be $9,000. Why didn't you add in the finance charge?" This is not their real question. Their real question is whether or not they are thoroughly convinced about the value of investing in your product, and to convince them may involve more selling. You see, it's been proven that buyer's remorse sets in more quickly when prospects are not reassured that they made the right decision.

And sometimes, even when prospects are reassured, they experience buyer's remorse, so your goal must be to continue to close. Now, more than ever, you must do everything in your power to get the situation back to where it once was in the closing sequence. Consider this stumbling block to be only temporary, and hang in there. Use all the techniques you know to keep you in the closing flow. Because you've invested so much time with these prospects, you may want to spend a few more minutes and try a few more things.

It helps to remember two things at this point: first, nothing ventured, nothing gained—the worst thing that can happen is that the prospects will end up saying No. And second, if that happens, remember that it's time to say "NEXT!" to yourself and start focusing on your next appointment.

Plenty of Fish in the Sea

As hard as might be to believe, you don't sell every lead or prospect you see. And the one you almost had on paper is by far the hardest one to lose. The situation is like that of the fisherman who tells the story of the one who got away. Sometimes you just have to bite the bullet, pack it up, and head on out of the prospects' home.

It also helps to be realistic and know that you'll get to do this same thing all over again with other prospects, too. You will go through an entire presentation to bring you back again to this point of the sale—or should I say no-sale.

Ease the Buyer

Let's go back briefly and review the doorknob close you learned about in the previous chapter. If you have done a doorknob close with clients, and in doing so have managed to bring them around to your way of thinking, remember that you need to spend some time warming them down. They balked once, and you shouldn't be surprised if they balk again.

You might start the warm-down process by asking for a glass of water. Put all your stuff away and talk about anything except the investment the prospects just made in your product. Talk about the weather, their family, their children, and their job, anything they are willing to discuss. Don't overstay your welcome, but sometime toward the end of the conversation, ask them if they feel good about their investment in your product. Ask them whether they have any remorse and whether are genuinely happy with the decision they've made.

Whatever they say, explain to them that their feelings are a natural reaction to the investment process, than proceed to tell them how they will feel when you leave. The interesting thing is that, if how they are going to feel is no surprise, they have more understanding of the situation. They can say, "He told me I would feel like this; it's normal, and I'm OK. Let me look a that brochure one more time. Oh, it really is beautiful! I can't wait to get it."

Keep in mind the idea that "It's not over till it's over." In other words, to PYI and solidify the close with prospects, you must warm them down and do everything in your power to address any concerns they still might have—*before* you walk out their door.

Replace the Lead

- **Protect Your Income, Ask for Referrals**

- **Write Name in Personal Directory**

- **3-6-9 Month Product Review**

- **Make Yourself Available**

- **Leave Magnetic Calling Card**

- **Get E-Mail Address**

- **Send Thank You Card**

- **Stay in Touch with Prospect**

STEP 10

Replace the Lead

STEP 1
Entry

STEP 2
Warm-up

STEP 3
Create Need

STEP 4
Company Story

STEP 5
Kill Options

STEP 6
Product Presentation

STEP 7
Pre-Close

STEP 8
Close

STEP 9
Post Close

STEP 10
Replace the Lead
Time of Sale
Time of Delivery
Keep in Touch

To get referrals, you must ask for referrals. Always try to replace the lead you're on with another two or three leads. This habit will separate you from the run-of-the-mill salesperson and make you a top-notch closer.

In every presentation you give, you should try to come out with two things. One of course is the sale, and the other is a number of referrals from the prospects you just gave the presentation to. You have earned the right to ask them for names of friends, family, or business associates.

Referrals: Warm Leads

The great thing about referrals is that they are *warm leads*. A warm lead is a lead in which the prospect has some idea about your product, has probably seen it work, has an idea of its cost, and has heard accolades about you and your company. If you gave me a referral lead every day, I would never complain—and I would be rich.

Ask and Ye Shall Receive (Well, Maybe)

A good way to find out who prospects know is to ask them—ask to receive. They might not remember any names immediately because they are under a tremendous amount of pressure, especially if they have just invested in your product. You know that old expression "I have it right here on the tip of my tongue." So sometimes, when you ask people this question about leads, they might lose their train of thought. And the harder they think, the less likely that they will come up with names. But there are some ways you can help them remember.

Get in Their Phone Directory

Ask to write your name and telephone number in the prospects' phone directory. Then when you're done, hand the directory back to them and ask them to leaf through it to jog their memory about other possible referrals—people they know who might be interested in receiving some information about what you have to offer.

If they happen to come up with names right away, ask if they think those persons would mind receiving some information about the product. Then go on to explain that sometimes when people receive information in the mail, they have a tendency to place it into the circular file cabinet commonly referred to as the trash can. Ask the prospects if they might introduce you over the telephone to the referrals, so you can ask them to watch out for your information package, to help ensure that it doesn't end up as garbage in some landfill.

The prospects hopefully will make that call, give you a grand testimonial over the phone, and then introduce you to the future prospects. Then, when you do go to the appointment, it will be as if you are old friends. What better way to start a business interview?

And the benefits don't stop there, either. If you really have learned about your prospects, you will know about the social events they participate in, whether those include their bowling league, the PTA, their church, or any other clubs.

Use the Referral Network

For prospects to participate in a referral network, you need to make it worthwhile to them. In other words, you must have some kind of referral program available. And above all, you must never renege on your commitment to pay prospects for their referrals.

You must always have something in writing to give to prospects that explains exactly how their referrals will be paid. Some people call this payment a *bird-dog fee* because prospects point you directly to other potential prospects. The key point is that you want to offer financial reward for prospects to earn when they provide you with other prospects. This arrangement represents seed planting at its finest. The only thing better than this is reaping what you sow.

I always say to the prospects I deal with:

> Mr. and Mrs. Prospect, we have a referral bonus program to present to you. It's not a get-rich-quick scheme, and you can't quit your job. It's just our way to say thank you for your business and for referring others to us. Let me explain to you how it works.

A Referral Bonus Program That Works

I believe in a bonus program to generate names that could lead to sales because it has one of the lowest lead costs. The referral delivers a high quality warm lead for a fraction of what you might pay to generate a quality lead in other ways.

If you ask for them properly, referrals keep work in your pipeline. Referrals are instant credibility because these prospects know you are reliable and won't rip them off. You are not really starting from scratch because prospects have some idea you are good at what you do or someone never would have referred you. Finally, referral jobs tend to be larger jobs than non-referral jobs.

Let me explain how the referral bonus program works in our business. We use a referral envelope that contains three coupons. The first coupon looks like currency in the amount of $100. The second coupon is for $150, and the third is for $200. Then we pay $200 for each referral after the third one. And we pay these amounts to people who turn us on to other potential prospects. We pay them this money when we deliver their product. I like to personally deliver this money to prospects because that gives me a chance to preach how well the referral system works. And besides, I like to give away money. And as I mentioned, relative to all the other ways we use to derive leads, this lead cost is quite inexpensive.

When Do I Ask For Referrals?

The best time to ask for referrals is right after you sign the sales contract. You have just spent hours selling yourself, your product, and your company. Everyone is excited for one reason or another. You are excited because you made the sale, the prospects are excited to get the product, and they think you're great. This is the golden opportunity to cash in and increase your business by getting referrals from prospects.

And there's no better time to ferret out or counter buyer's remorse. You have made the sale, and now you are asking your clients to turn you on to their friends and family. Their doing so is definitely reinforcement for you, and it also demonstrates that they invested in your product of their own free will.

Give to Get Referrals Later

Few people will refuse you referrals at the time of the sale. But to get referrals from them on subsequent visits, you must set the stage. To do this, when you go back to the prospects' house, you start by saying, "Mr. and Mrs. Prospect, I know you have names for me, and I will get those names in a little while. But first, how do you like the product? Any complaints?" Use this time to discuss the product with them and answer any questions or concerns they might have. Then continue, "So how many of you're friends and relatives have seen the product?" This gives them a chance to think about the people they have come in contact with who also might be interested in your product. You are just jogging their memory. They will remember that they agreed to supply you with names earlier. And as you did before, if they do give you names, it's a good idea to ask them to call and introduce you to those people over the telephone.

Excuses Satisfy Only Their Makers

Too many sales people are afraid to ask for referrals because they have this false sense that they might jeopardize the business relationship they have with the current prospect. But if they don't ask, they will never receive.

I have always believed that excuses satisfy only those who make them. If you want to sit around and rationalize why you don't get referrals, doing so is entirely up to you. But I will say you are costing yourself a lot of money by not creating leads through referrals.

Consider these examples the next time you begin to tell yourself that prospects don't want to give you referrals:

- I receive calls from satisfied customers, and I sometimes ask them why they haven't referred someone to us. They often say they have never been asked to do that.

- A potential prospect calls into the office and says, "Mr. and Mrs. Whatever referred us, and we would like to have someone stop out and give us an estimate." This tells me that a sales representative is not following up with previous customers to get referrals. He or she should have been in contact with these prospects before they phoned in.

The point is this: You need to get in the habit of asking for referrals in the right way and at the best time. You will find that most people have plenty of referrals, and they are eager to give them to you if only you will ask.

If you secure one referral a month, which represents 12 sales a year, and multiply each of those prospects by your average sale and again by your commission rate, the result equals found money. These referrals will provide you with money that never would have been there without your extra effort to get names.

Remember that we are all creatures of habit. To change or modify your behavior, you must always ask prospects for referrals—on every call, every sale, and every no-sale.

Keep Lists of Past Customers

One way to get immediate satisfaction out of your referral program is to get a list of your past customers. If you haven't done this

SALES PRO TIP

Don't Leave Them Alone—Get on the Phone
Develop the habit of keeping lists of customers you've closed, and then calling them after the sale to thank them for their business and ask them for referrals of other good prospects like themselves.

before, you might feel awkward at first. Next, get each former customer on the phone. You must be very honest when you say:

> Mr. or Mrs. Prospect, the reason for my call is that I really want to thank you for putting your trust in me. I'm so glad I had a chance to work with you. I'm trying to build up my business. You people were a pleasure to deal with, and I'm trying to find people similar to you. My question is "Do you know any people who might be interested in receiving a packet describing the benefits of my product?" It's easier to work with people like yourselves than to call people who don't know me.

The success of this approach is contingent on your relationship with those prospects. Some will have to think about it and get back to you. Others will immediately give you names and organizations you might want to call. Next, you'll want to put a packet together to send to the people they refer to you, and then follow up with those new prospects.

Remember Service, Not Product

When I asked one of my sales representatives why he didn't get referrals, he told me that it's too much like begging. I immediately countered with this:

> Look, James, you need to change your mindset. You are providing a valuable service to people. You really aren't selling anything. You are just getting names so these people will come to you when they are ready. All I'm asking you to do is make yourself ready. You want to make sure that, should they ever develop an interest in your product, you will be the first person they call—not your competitor.

SALES PRO TIP

You're Not Selling Products. You're Providing a Service.
To help overcome any reluctance to ask for referrals, remember that you're just preparing to offer your services to people when they're ready—you're not selling anything.

Join Your PTA for Leads

You can become affiliated with many organizations. Most referrals come from meeting people. To become better known among the people you come into contact with, become active in your community. Let these people know what you do for a living and the kind of product you sell.

One of the best organizations I have found to become associated with is the PTA. I suggest that you join your local PTA or other parent-teacher organization as quickly as you can, especially if you have children. This is such a great group to network with because the people you come into contact with all have children, and are generally open and willing to talk to you. In practical terms, the people who attend these functions also typically are active in their community, have sufficient money, and have plenty of contact with other people who may have money.

This method of developing referrals is a no-nonsense approach that is both time- and cost-effective. Developing such contacts evolves over time, like rolling a small snowball in the snow until it becomes a larger snowball and eventually a snowman. Another neat thing about these prospects is that they call you, and my experience confirms that prospects developed this way are far less price-sensitive than prospects you might find otherwise.

The Triangle Method

Although you might dislike canvassing neighborhoods, it is still wise to visit your previous customers and use what is called the *tri-*

SALES PRO TIP

Use the Triangle Method to Canvas Previous Customers
Visit previous customers, and their neighbors on the right, the left, and across the street, to develop new leads.

angle method to develop new prospects. The triangle method involves visiting the houses to the right and the left of your customers' home, and the house across the street from them. Make sure your customers know you're coming, and they might even introduce you to their neighbors.

Again, they will do this if you provide a paid referral fee for those live bodies, which can lead to sales. And to keep in mind how important such referrals are, consider this: I know sales representatives who have been in the sales game a long time and who live off their referrals—they get so many referrals that they need no other form of leads to earn a decent living.

Testimonial Letters Revisited

Another way to develop sales is to use testimonial letters from previous customers. Any time your prospects praise you after your product is delivered, make sure you immediately ask them to "say it in writing"—would they please write a testimonial letter? Carry all the testimonial letters in one book and hand the book to the prospects you're talking with. Make arrangements with the people included in the testimonial book that, if they allow future prospects to call them as a reference for you and your product, you will "bird dog" them with referral money.

Testimonial letters are not a time-consuming project; they take just moments for you to arrange if you are only willing to do it. Once again, when you get into the habit, getting testimonial letters will

SALES PRO TIP

Ask for Orphaned Accounts
Another way to gain referrals is to go to orphaned accounts for them. An orphaned account used to belong to a sales representative who is no longer working with the company. Go to these customers, introduce yourself as the representative who will now be handling their accounts, and proceed to ask for referrals.

become second nature, and they will provide you with ample leads to sustain yourself through the rough times when other lead sources dry up.

A Lead Is a Lead Is a Lead

A lead is a lead is a lead, and nothing more. You must develop it, cultivate it, harvest it, and above all, close it. To make money, you need to be in front of people. You must be demonstrating your product. And if you are in front of people and not demonstrating, then you are not selling.

The people with the highest demonstration rate generally have the highest closing statistics and make the most money. That is why I have written down on a sheet of paper in my car (remember this?), "Nothing a customer will say or do will keep me from giving a full and complete product demonstration."

Become a Professional Visitor

Here again, one last time, is the idea of using sayings or words of wisdom for encouragement to remain successful at developing leads—and at selling. As long as the words are positive motivation, where they come from doesn't matter. The words to remember this time are to consider yourself a professional visitor.

For example, I have to a certain degree become a professional visitor in my sales career. The people who I visit are the people who have displayed trust and faith in me in the past—my previous customers. I will make a least two stops a day to make my presence felt and to let my past customers know I want some names of people they know who have seen the product and are willing to receive some information.

You now know about several approaches you can take to replace the lead—to develop one or more new prospects from the information you get from your current and former prospects and clients. Remember, to replace the lead is to succeed.

Glossary

assumptive close   The theory that the hardest word in the human language to say is no. The assumptive close means pulling out a contract and starting to write. If they don't say a word, assume the silence as a go ahead with the sale.

Better Business Bureau (BBB)   A consumer can find the longevity of any company.

buyer's remorse   Dilemma the consumer puts themselves into by purchasing something they no longer believe they want or need, much less can afford.

buying signals   Statements made by the prospect giving you indication that they plan on purchasing the product.

close   Closing the sale is the natural conclusion to the successful implementation of the selling plan.

confidence selling   Plays an important role in the competitive market place. The one who is thoroughly convincing will win the prospect over and gain their business and earn their trust.

Consumer Protection Agencies   Consumers can file complaints to this agency, letter usually informs company they have 10 days to rectify the problem.

disposable product   It feels cheap, it's made cheap, it looks cheap, and it's cheap to buy.

entry   First walk up to the prospect's door.

FAB System   Features, Advantages, and Benefits system.

future pacing   Tell the prospect exactly what is going to happen before it happens.

geared selling presentation   Explaining things in a sequence or certain order helps to tell the story in a way the prospect can relate to.

name recognition   Selling a product that is a great product, will cause people to tell other people. Soon your product will be a brand name.

objections   Signals given by the consumer that come across as stalls. "Not interested, Can not afford, Do not need, Not ready yet, Your product is not what I want, and Your price is too high.

permanent product   Permanent solution to the problems you now encounter.

picture portfolio   To show your product in use

Positive Mental Attitude (PMA)   The single thing that will help you accomplish whatever it is you want to accomplish out of life.

pre-close   The pre-close involves working out the retail price quote, working out a budget for the prospect and setting up urgency as a reason for them to do business with your company today.

price conditioning   Important process in order to establish product worth.

product demonstration   Highlighting all the features, advantages, and benefits of your product. This demonstration must include a group of sample cases with a breakdown of your product inside.

prospect   The customer.

referral network   The prospect will earn for providing you with other prospects.

right of recession   Gives the prospect three days to cancel the contract.

testimonial letters   Letters from previous customers that are satisfied with your product.

third party influence   Comes from magazines, newspaper articles, or anything that is in print from creditable and reliable sources. Preferably these print items are from well-known people or publications.

word target response   Again utilization of qualifiers getting the prospect accustomed to saying Yes is so vitally important. All qualifying questions should be geared to produce a Yes response.